To Nick O'Reilly:

With best wishes.

Richard Renstrow

7/18/81

MOTORCYCLE MILESTONES

MOTORCYCLE MILESTONES

Volume I

by

Richard Renstrom

ACKNOWLEDGMENTS

I AM INDEBTED to many people who have helped me in my research and photographic work on this book. Many sources have also helped by providing some of the black and white photographs used in this book. I would, therefore, like to express my appreciation to the following, some of whom are sadly no longer in business.

The British magazine *Motor Cycle,* BMW, FN, Royal Enfield, Husqvarna, Moto Guzzi, Gilera, Montesa, Norton, NSU, DOT, Harley-Davidson, Zweitakt Motorrad Museum, Triumph, BSA, Honda, CZ, Jawa, the Ariel Owners Motorcycle Club, Sears-Roebuck, Frank Conley of CAMA, Matchless, Maico, MV Agusta, Ducati, AJS, Puch, Bultaco, and many members of the Antique Motorcycle Club of America. And perhaps, most of all, I need to thank my wife, Betty Jean, who for nearly 20 years has faithfully critiqued my manuscripts and typed them into final form. Without her help and support, none of this would have been possible.

Richard Renstrom
April 1, 1980

THE AUTHOR

THE AUTHOR of nearly 800 feature articles in magazines all over the world, Richard Renstrom is one of the world's ranking historians of motorcycle sport. A writer since 1963, Dick regularly has his work published in the leading car and motorcycle magazines in America, Australia, England, Holland, France, Germany, Italy, Sweden, and Switzerland.

Dick's first book, *Motorsport On Two Wheels,* was published by Cycle World in 1970, which was followed by *Motorrad Rennsport* in 1972 by Motorbuch Verlag in Germany. Next came *The Great Motorcycles* by Bond-Parkhurst Publishing Company in 1972, followed by his best selling *Great Motorcycle Legends* by Haessner Publishing Company in 1977.

The result of a ten year effort to photograph one hundred of the most significant motorcycles in the history of the sport, *Motorcycle Milestones* is intended to be a four volume series. This new book combines the art of photography with the author's historical knowledge to produce what he feels is his finest work to date.

The author lives in Caldwell, Idaho, where he manages Classics Unlimited, which deals exclusively in classic and antique motorcycles. Dick enjoys restoring vintage motorcycles himself, and he has won many concours trophies with bikes from his own collection.

The author is also the founder of the West Coast Velocette Club and the Idaho Vintage Motorcycle Club. Dick served two years as president of both clubs, as well as president of the MG Classics Car Club in Idaho. The recipient of many awards for his work, the author has served as president of the Idaho Writers League and was appointed by the Governor to the first Idaho Arts and Humanities Commission in 1966.

Contents

THE MOTORCYCLE —
Its Birth and Development

THE MODERN MOTORCYCLE is a remarkable machine. Beautiful, fast, and sophisticated, it offers the ultimate in mechanical perfection, economical and reliable transportation, and sport. There was once a time, however, when man depended upon his own muscles or the muscles of a horse to get him where he wished to go. Then along came the steam engine in the early 1800s to provide steam powered ships and trains, followed by the bicycle in the middle 1800s that gave a great boost to human muscle power.

It was not until 1876 that the age of mechanized power really began, however, since that was the year when Dr. N. A. Otto of Deutz, Germany patented the first practical internal combustion engine. Otto's four-stroke engine was followed in 1881 by Sir Dugald Clerk's two-stroke design in which the incoming fuel charge was sucked into the crankcase and then pressured into the combustion chamber via a set of transfer ports.

These two primitive powerplants set many minds to thinking. If this newfangled form of power could just be harnessed to a common bicycle, man would at last have a form of transportation with nearly unlimited potential.

Many inventive minds went to work on the idea in both Europe and America, with the honor of creating the world's first true motorcycle going to Gottlieb Daimler in Canstatt, Germany. Daimler's crude motorcycle rolled out of his shop in 1885 as an impractical and unreliable proposition, but it did prove to everyone that the concept had merit. The motorcycle had been born.

Gottlieb's invention was followed in 1887 by Frenchman Emile Levassor's motorcycle in which a clutch was used to disengage the engine, which was followed in 1894 by the Hildebrand & Wolfmuller — the world's first commercially produced motorbike. This German machine was still very crude, however, and had exposed connecting rods working on a "live" rear axle. In the following three years about 800 models were produced, and then the company went out of business.

This 1910 Racycle well illustrates the belt drives and pull-back handlebars so popular in the early days.

Meanwhile, in America, many inventors had been busy trying to produce a practical motorcycle, with the Pennington Company of Racine, Wisconsin designing a motorbike in 1895 that featured a "hot air" engine which burned kerosene and turned over at 500 rpm. The Pennington design also had the engine's connecting rods working directly on the rear axle, which helped along its early demise to the history books.

Perhaps the most significant thing in America occurred in 1899 when a Brooklyn tool and die maker named Oscar Hedstrom showed up with a gasoline-engined bicycle to pace early-day bicycle races. In January of 1900 the Swedish born inventor took his motorbike to the famous Madison Square Garden arena to pace the bicycles, where he caught the eye of bicycle producing king, George Hendee. Hendee was visibly impressed with Hedstrom's invention, and he soon made a deal with Hedstrom to join him in a partnership to design and produce America's first motorcycle.

Hedstrom went right to work on improving his design, with the first prototype being completed in the spring of 1901. The public was invited to the initial demonstration, which took place in Springfield, Massachusetts. The motorbike performed to perfection, and Hedstrom was able to climb a rather steep hill. Being a man of exceptional vision, Hendee saw great possibilities for a motorized bicycle, so he quickly formed the Hendee Manufacturing Company and began production.

The name given the new motorcycle was "Indian," and thus was born America's first motorcycle that would, in time, become a legend. In fairness to history we must mention that other Yankee inventors had also designed and sold some motorbikes by then, but it remained for Hedstrom and Hendee to actually produce the first models for sale in any real numbers.

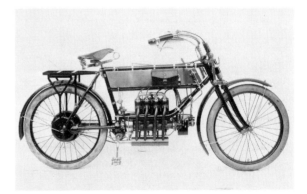
The Belgian FN Company marketed the world's first four-cylinder motorcycle in 1905. This is a 1910 500cc model.

The powerplant used for these first Indians was a single-cylinder engine from the Aurora Company in Illinois. In 1901 Indian produced just three machines, but in 1902 a total of 143 machines rolled off the lines. In 1903 production was up to 377, and then in 1904 a total of 546 units were produced. Indian went on to sell 31,950 machines in 1913 and a peak of 41,000 in 1916 — making them the largest manufacturer in the world with exports to dozens of foreign countries.

These first Indians were more reliable than most for those early days, which encouraged the company to add a 5 HP V-twin to their range for 1906. A pair of these twins were then ridden from coast to coast, which was a remarkable achieve-

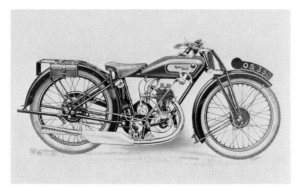

This 1924 Royal Enfield is typical of British design then with a side-valve engine and three-speed, hand-shifted gearbox.

ment over the rough dirt roads. Indian also obtained some great publicity when George Holden won America's first road race — a 10 miler in Brooklyn.

Europe, meanwhile, had also been busy, with brothers Michel and Eugene Werner producing a motorbike in 1897 that had a small motor clipped to the front fork. A belt drive was used to the front wheel with no method of disengagement. The brothers followed this up in 1901 with their "New Werner," a machine that had the engine centrally mounted in the frame. The last New Werners were produced in 1908.

By 1905 the European scene was alight with dozens of motorbike producing companies. Most of these early-day models used single-cylinder, four-stroke engines of one to four horsepower, but a few used the two-stroke design. Virtually all of them used a direct belt drive to the rear wheel, with no method of disengaging the engine from the wheel. Braking power was provided on only the rear wheel, with either a bicycle-type coaster brake in the hub or a caliper brake on the wheel rim or belt rim.

The four-stroke engine was still in its infancy then and featured an overhead intake valve and side exhaust valve. The exhaust valve was mechanically opened by a cam, but the intake valve had just a low-poundage spring to hold it

The Swedish Husqvarna Company produced this "Specialracer Motorcykel" in 1930. The 500cc JAP powered single was used in road racing and cross-country races.

shut and depended on the piston travel to suck it open or push it closed. During the years of 1906 to 1908 a trend began in Europe to operate the intake valve by a cam and pushrod-rocker arm setup, which was copied by Indian in 1908 and the American Harley-Davidson in 1911.

The American scene also came alive then with dozens of companies getting into the act. The most successful was Harley-Davidson — founded in

Milwaukee, Wisconsin in 1903 by brothers Arthur, Walter, and William Davidson and William S. Harley. Their first motorcycle was a 27 cubic inch, 3 HP single with belt drive, which was ridden by a series of owners no less than 83,000 miles. Harley-Davidson thus staked out their reputation on reliability rather than speed or sophisticated

Ernst Henne set a new world speed record in 1934 of 152.81 mph with this 750cc BMW that featured an early attempt at streamlining.

technology — a philosophy that has continued to this day.

In the decade just prior to World War I, motorcycling became very popular in America. By 1911 more than 100 makes were in existance, with many companies existing for just a few short years. Some of the most notable were Yale, Marsh, Col-

The Italian Moto Guzzi Company produced some replica racers in the late 1930s for the private owners. This is a 250cc Albatross model.

9

umbia, Thor, Curtiss, Marvel, Merkel, AMC, Thomas, Orient, Excelsior, Apache, Pope, Pierce, Ivor-Johnson, Holley, Cleveland, Henderson, Ace, Minneapolis, Cyclone, Monarch, Champion, Eagle, Arrow, Dayton, and many others including a steam-engined model by John Barr in Middleton, Ohio.

Several mail-order firms also got into the act, with Sears-Roebuck and Montgomery-Ward both selling motorbikes. Motorcycle racing soon became the rage, and dozens of steeply banked board tracks sprang up around the country. State and county fairs staged races on their one-half and one-mile dirt tracks, and the crowds flocked to see the fire-belching beasts perform.

Indian was the racing champion during the early days, but Excelsior, Merkel, and Thor soon put up factory teams and the competition became torrid.

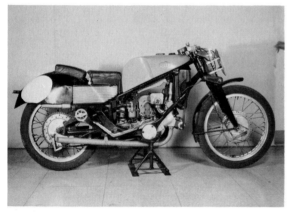

The terror of the 1939 grand prix scene was this supercharged four-cylinder Gilera-Rondine. The water-cooled four ran nearly 150 mph.

Harley had chosen to ignore the racing game at first, but the huge crowds and resultant publicity soon forced them to get involved. In 1914 the first H-D factory racing team appeared, and within a few years their riders were nearly unbeatable on their fast 8-valve 1000cc V-twins. The rivalry between the teams was fierce, with the finest riders

being paid huge salaries to bring home the trophies.

These early works racers were overhead valve models with open exhaust ports or short exhaust pipes. Running on alcohol fuel they were fast and noisy, which helped them create a spectacle of speed that captivated America. Motorcycling was in its greatest hour and sales expanded to dizzy heights.

The greatest American racing victory was not achieved in the United States, however, but rather across the seas on the Isle of Man, just off the west coast of England. The Isle of Man first hosted a Tourist Trophy Race in 1907 over a 15 mile course, which was expanded in 1911 to a 37-1/2 mile circuit that went clear around the island and took in a 1350 foot climb from sea level to well up on Snaefell Mountain. Dozens of corners were included, plus many uphill and downhill sections, which made it the most demanding road racing course in the world. The great tradition of the "TT" was thus born, which quickly became the most prestigious and famous road racing event in the world.

This twisty and hilly road was a bit tough on single speed, belt drive motorbikes, which lacked a lower gear for the steeper sections and also suffered from belt slip. Indian, however, felt they had

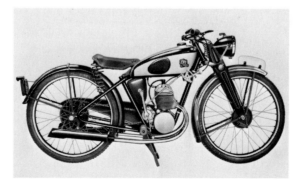

Spain entered the world of motorcycle production in 1946 with this 98cc Montesa two-stroke single. Montesa now specializes in dirt bikes.

a vastly superior design in their IOE twin with a two-speed countershaft gearbox and clutch — an idea they had first used on their 1910 models. Indian did have a racing 8-valve V-twin then for their factory riders, but the rules for the TT required that standard touring models be used.

Indian sent five bikes to the Island along with ace rider Jake De Rosier, who retired after leading the first lap. When the flag fell on the 187 mile race, Indian had a 1-2-3 win, with Oliver Godfrey averaging 47.6 mph. This stunning victory prompted the British Matchless concern to challenge De Rosier to a three race matchup at the fast Brooklands concrete bowl, with both sides using their 1000cc OHV works racers. Jake blew a tire in one race but won the other two over Charlie Collier, one heat at 84.5 mph. With these two great wins

The 1950 Norton Manx was produced in 350 and 500cc sizes. This DOHC single featured the old style plunger rear suspension and a 115 mph speed.

behind them, Indian triumphantly returned to America where they led their country to an even greater technical lead over the Europeans for the following dozen years.

During the 1905 to 1925 era the American manufacturers were blessed with tremendous sales and a public that was passionately interested in motorcycles. This provided the profits to support an aggressive research program, which resulted in many models of exceptional excellence.

Indian pioneered the chain drive right from their beginning, and they also pioneered a mechanical oil pump in 1910 that provided more positive lubrication than the common gravity feed system. In 1913 they introduced a spring frame model to help smooth out the rough roads, and then in 1916 they introduced their 1000cc Powerplus model with a side-valve engine in which the valve gear was totally enclosed — thus keeping the oil inside the engine and off the rider. The Powerplus also had a 3-speed gearbox, as did the 1915 Harley.

The British, meanwhile, were playing around with two and even three speed models, with the gears and often the clutch located in the rear hub. They also changed from the IOE engine design to the side-valve design in the 1908 to 1912 era, but typically left the valvesprings exposed.

The Americans clearly led the world in speed, however, with Eugene Walker setting the first official F.I.M. World speed record of 103.95 mph on his 61 inch Indian in 1920, which was followed by

The German NSU concern used their pre-war road racing bike to set a new speed record of 180 mph in 1951 and 211 mph in 1956. The supercharged twin featured a full shell and 110 HP from the 500cc engine.

Red Wolverton's 129 mph clocking in 1923 on his Ace four-cylinder model. America's last great effort came in 1926, when Johnny Seymour rocketed through the traps at 132.0 mph on his 61 inch Indian 8-valve twin and 115.64 on a 4-valve

500cc single — speeds that were well beyond anything being recorded in Europe.

On the steeply banked board tracks the speeds recorded by these 8-valve twins bordered on the incredulous and made European track speeds seem like child's play. The 110 mph lap record was broken in 1922 by Jim Davis, who then did 113 mph in 1926 at Altoona, Pennsylvania. Curley Fredrichs set the all time lap record for the boards in 1928 with a 120.3 mph speed at Salem, New Hampshire — a speed that staggered the Europeans.

The British DOT was a pioneer of the two-stroke in moto-cross racing. This 1951 200cc model won many 250cc class races then.

The Europeans were torn apart by World War I, but by 1920 they resumed production and quickly applied the technology of war to peacetime use. First came the new overhead value engine with a hemispherical combustion chamber, which provided a great boost in revs and power. Next came good internal expanding brakes, followed in the late twenties by a fuel tank that was mounted over the top frame rails instead of between them. A front brake was added in the early 1920s, which was copied by Indian and H-D in 1928.

By the middle 1920s, motorcycling had passed its peak in America. Mass production methods were being used then to produce cars so cheaply that the people could afford automobiles. In this

age of rapidly expanding affluence, everyone could have the prestige of a car, which cut into motorcycle sales drastically. Sales tumbled, and so did profits. Without profits the money wasn't there to finance a racing program, so that manufacturer support dropped to nothing. Design progress came to a halt, and the golden days were over.

In Europe the motorcycle was enjoying tremendous popularity. Grand prix road racing became terribly important then, and a great deal of what was learned on the track was applied to the standard roadsters. In 1926 England clearly took the lead when a 350cc Velocette won the Junior TT — the first TT win by an overhead camshaft engine. Velocette then showed up with a positive-stop, foot shift-and-hand clutch on their 1928 TT models — an idea which was soon adopted by the entire British industry.

The economic depression of the early 1930s slowed things down a bit in Europe, but by 1935 sales were up again and technical progress reached a fever pitch. Aided by a formal European

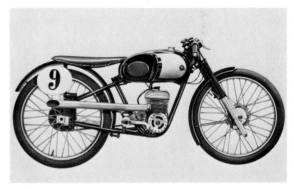

Montesa entered this 125cc road racer in 1949 grand prix events, but two-stroke technology was not competitive then with the four-strokes.

Championship, road racing became a tremendous spectacle with up to 250,000 fans at the major grands prix. Much of the knowledge gained from road racing was applied to the standard roadsters — a practice that was especially true in England.

A great deal of attention was focused then on making the motorcycle more comfortable to ride. While there had been some notable spring frame models in the early days (the 1909 Merkel, 1913 Indian, and 1920 Nimbus, Denmark), all of these had been classified as failures, due probably to the weak frame tubes flexing and thus causing poor handling. The big breakthrough finally came in 1928 when both the British Vincent and the Italian

In 1952 Harley-Davidson produced their first model with a foot shift and swinging-arm rear suspension. This 750cc K model had a side-valve engine.

Moto Guzzi produced models with a pivoted fork rear suspension. Neither had the benefit of hydraulic damping, but the frames were strong enough then to resist flexing so that the handling was not suspect.

Guzzi raced with passion then and hired the great Irish rider, Stanley Woods, to pilot their 250cc single and 500cc V-twin in the Lightweight and Senior TTs. Stanley proceeded to win both and set an 86.53 mph lap record in the Senior event, which motivated most of the factories to design a rear suspension system for their 1936 works racers. The plunger type became the most popular, but the most significant was the modern swinging-arm design on the works Velocettes, which was then used in 1939 on the 350cc replica KTT model.

The German BMW was also a pioneer in those days, with their opposed twin engine and shaft drive offering an exceptionally smooth power delivery. In 1935 BMW introduced a telescopic front fork, which gained hydraulic damping in 1936 on the 500cc OHV R5 model. BMW also used this type of fork on their works racers, as did Norton in 1938.

During the middle 1930s the European machines nearly all adopted a four speed gearbox, and this plus powerful OHV and OHC engines provided an outstanding performance. By the late 1930s many companies produced models for touring, sporting road use, scrambles, trials, and road racing. England was clearly in the lead then and exported thousands of machines all over the world.

During the late 1930s the grand prix scene reached a fever pitch. Technical progress was at the greatest rate ever achieved, which was aided by government financial support in Italy and Germany. Supercharging was allowed under the F.I.M. rules then, so that the speeds became as-

Rene Baeten of Belgium won the 1958 world moto-cross championship on this 500cc FN that weighed 350 pounds. FN no longer produces motorcycles.

tounding. In 1939, for instance, the 500cc BMW was churning out 68 HP at 8000 rpm for a 140 mph speed, while the championship-winning Gilera-Rondine "four" from Italy was clocking nearly 150 mph. The British Norton and Velocette

singles fought back gamely with superb handling and 125 mph speeds, but they were just too slow.

In the 350cc class the 117 mph Velocettes barely edged out the blown DKW two-stroke from Germany, which featured a four-piston design with two combustion chambers. The supercharged DKW 250cc split-single won its class, just as it had since 1935. It was an incredible international battle with many makes and many designs — the most classic year the sport has ever known.

Meanwhile, in America, things weren't going very well. Motorcycling had sunk into obscurity, with only Harley and Indian surviving the terrible depression. Huge and clumsy 750 to 1300cc side-valve twins were the order of the day, which featured awkward 3-speed, hand shift-and-foot clutch systems. Very reliable, but not very exciting. Harley did produce a 61 inch OHV model with a 4-speed transmission in 1936, but with a 600 pound weight it was really not very progressive. This lack of progress in America was most apparent in the lubrication systems, which were still the total-loss type until 1932 on the Indians and 1936-37 on the Harleys. Dumping the used oil onto the road was not the cutting edge of technical progress in 1935!

The American racing formula also reflected this design stagnation of the 1930s. Neither H-D nor Indian could afford to design and build exotic rac-

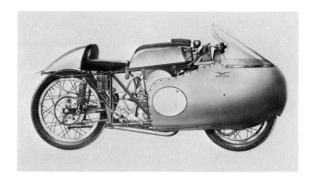

Moto Guzzi raced this 350cc single in 1955 with great success. The full "dustbin" fairings were outlawed by the F.I.M. at the end of the 1957 season.

ing models, so a new "Class C" formula replaced the "Class A" rules in 1933 in which 750cc side-valve production models or 500cc OHV models were allowed. In addition, the OHV models were limited to a 7.0 to 1 compression ratio — a move aimed at reducing the threat of the well designed OHV and OHC bikes from England. The American scene thus sunk further into stagnation and obscurity.

Then came World War II, and everyone forgot about the peacetime use of motorcycles. England was back in production in 1946, and, with a great need for income from foreign sources to help rebuild their war-torn land, the British placed a great emphasis on developing export sales. There was a great demand everywhere then for all types of

The first post-war two-stroke capable of beating the four-strokes was the 1956 DKW 350cc "three" that developed 45 HP at 9700 rpm and ran 145 mph.

motor vehicles, of course, since there had been few cars or bikes sold to the public during the war years. An added bonus to England was the hundreds of thousands of American soldiers who had sampled the light and peppy British bikes during the war. This created a ready market in America for this new breed of bike that handled and performed so well, which opened up a glorious new era of motorcycle sport in America. Motorcycling

was once again fun, and a whole new concept of motorcycle sport unfolded in the United States.

The British machines of the early post-war years were basically their 1939 models, but by 1948 all of England's manufacturers had dropped the old girder front fork in favor of the new telescopic type that offered increased rider comfort. Spring frames became a popular option then, which was enhanced in 1949 when AJS, Matchless, and Royal Enfield offered swinging-arm models in their catalogue. Norton and Velocette followed in 1953, as did BSA and Triumph in 1954.

The British were also aided by the F.I.M.'s post-war ban on superchaging, which put the 350cc KTT Velocette and 500cc Manx Norton right back at the top of the racing scene, along with the Moto Guzzi and Benelli 250cc singles from Italy. Moto-cross racing, which had been tried before the war, became popular then, and the British factories were soon producing specialized models for moto-cross, trials, road racing, and sports road use (high performance Club-

Perhaps the most beautiful moto-cross bike of all time was the 1960-63 Husqvarna 500cc single that used a modified 1935 roadster engine from Albin.

man racers), as well as an exceptionally fine range of single, twin, and four-cylinder touring models. England was the undisputed leader in sales, design, and sport, with her factories exporting their wares to every corner of the globe.

This British superiority was also evident in America, where they now outsold the domestic manufacturers. They also achieved their fourth consecutive win by a Norton Manx in the prestigious Daytona Beach 200 Mile National Championship in 1952, when English bikes took the first sixteen places.

During this period the great name of Indian passed from the scene when the illustrious factory closed its doors early in 1953. The great pioneer, the creative genius of the early days, was no more.

Harley-Davidson fought back with a radically new 750cc (45 inch) K model in 1952 that had the rather obsolete side-valve engine mounted in a swinging-arm frame with a telescopic front fork, plus a new four-speed, foot-shifted gearbox to replace the three-speed, hand-shifted W model. A much faster machine, this supposedly ancient design was then patiently developed by the race shop until it was capable of lapping the outer bowl at Daytona at 150 mph — an incredible performance for a flathead design! These last side-valve twins then faded from the American tracks at the end of the 1969 season when the formula was changed to allow 750cc OHV and OHC models. They went out in a blaze of vintage glory, though, with Mert Lawwill etching his name into the history books as national champion on a flathead Harley.

History was made in 1959 when Roy Peplow won the Scottish Six Days Trial on this 200cc Triumph single. This was the first win by a "lightweight."

During the late 1950s and early 1960s the British quietly abandoned their now classic singles to concentrate on 500 and 650cc twins, although the singles still ruled supreme for road racing, trials, and moto-cross. The continental scene came alive then also, with the sales lead taken away from England by Germany and Italy, where 50cc mopeds and 100 to 250cc lightweights became the rage. With superb engineering and often overhead cams, these high revving buzz bombs were sold by the millions.

Due, perhaps, to the ever increasing tax burden placed upon the British people to support an elaborate social welfare state plus a tax system that was punitive towards capital formation, design progress seemed to stagnate. The labor unions also acquired a power that hindered effective business management, which effectively slowed the creative genius of the British Industry. The industry that had been so innovative during the 1925 to 1955 era seemed suddenly to have become very tired. One by one the great names of the past went broke until, by 1976, only Triumph remained — and this grand old company was occupied by a workers' co-operative that required government financing to remain afloat!

Meanwhile, on the other side of the world, Japan was struggling to rebuild a country devastated by war. It took a few years to get things back to normal, but by the late 1950s the Japanese were beginning to make themselves felt in the international markets. One of the items they were trying to produce was motorcycles. Their first efforts were pitiful — about like a German machine of the early 1930s, but by 1960 Honda had some 50cc singles and 125cc twins of a unique design that enabled them to get a foothold in America and other foreign countries. Next came the Honda 250cc Hawk and 305cc Super Hawk in 1962, which had OHC twin-cylinder engines of an advanced design plus a 103 mph top speed in the 305cc size. A reliable machine that sold at a price well below the American and European machines,

the new breed of Oriental motorcycle sold in great numbers.

Honda also became involved in grand prix racing in 1959 in the TT and drew little response but laughs, only to return in 1960 with 125cc twins and 250cc fours that performed respectably well. Using computorized technology to help design their machines, Honda returned in 1961 and stood Europe on its ear with a stunning demonstration of speed that brought them two world championships. The Japanese industry has never looked back, and today they dominate the world

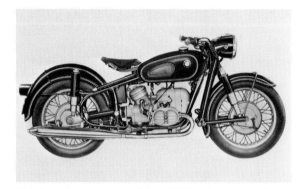

BMW introduced a new model in 1955 that featured a swinging arm suspension both front and rear. This is a 1965 500cc model.

scene with sales in the millions and racing records by the book full.

Another significant achievement of the 1960s was the rise of the two-stroke design. With research into port design and the expansion-box exhaust system, DKW in Germany fielded a competitive 350cc three-cylinder roadracer in 1955, which was followed by the 125 and 250cc MZs from East Germany in the late 1950s and early 1960s that never won a world championship but did win many grand prix races. Ernst Degner finally won a championship in 1962 with his 50cc two-stroke Suzuki, which was followed by a classic MV Agusta versus two-stroke battle until 1975, at which time the great Italian four-stroke proponent

finally lost heart and faded away to give the two-strokes a total domination of the sport. Very fast, but to many the contemporary road racing scene has lost its technical interest.

In trials and moto-cross there was also an epic battle between the two designs, but when the legendary Sammy Miller stepped off his 1964 Scottish Six Days Trial winning 500cc Ariel to ride a 250cc Bultaco to victory in 1965, the era of classic four-stroke bog wheels came to an end. In moto-cross the great Jeff Smith took world championships in both 1964 and 1965 on his 441cc BSA single, but then Paul Friedrichs beat Smith in 1966 on his 360cc CZ to halt the reign of the four-stroke scrambles bikes that had endured since the 1930s. Another era was ended.

The story of the motorcycle is thus a fascinating epic of many minds and many designs. Born in Germany in 1885, the technical lead came to America in the early years of this century until being assumed by the British in the middle 1920s. The English era was long and classic and lasted until the middle 1950s, at which time continental Europe took the lead until the Japanese came to dominate the world in the early 1960s.

As with most complex technologies, the modern

Honda first made their name with small 50cc models in both Japan and in America. First came the road models, followed by trail models such as this 1966 90cc single.

motorcycle was not invented in one grand swoop, but was rather a process of one brilliant mind building upon the ideas, success, and failures of those who came before him. The evolution of the motorcycle is thus a product of many minds from every corner of the earth — a beautiful and colorful story that continues to this day. The golden oldies of the past are thus a treasured piece of humanity and man's progress on earth — a treasure of aesthetic excellence, engineering, sport, and history that only grows richer with each passing year.

The last great British single was the Velocette, last produced in 1971. This is a 500cc Thruxton model — a 110 mph pseudo-roadracer.

The last win by a four-stroke single in world championship moto-cross was in 1965 when Jeff Smith took the title on this 441cc BSA single.

Since 1964 when Joel Robert won the world 250cc championship, the CZ from Czechoslovakia has been a contender for the moto-cross title. This is a 1966 360cc model.

Honda set the world on fire in 1969 with their new 750cc four-cylinder model that would run 125 mph. Very sophisticated with electric starting.

1898 Ariel 500cc Motor Tricycle
England

IN THE REALLY EARLY DAYS of the motorcycle, before 1900, there was by no means any agreement on where the engine should be mounted on the bicycle. Some thought the front was the best place, while others liked the rear fender. Still others mounted the motor on one of the wheels.

One of those who thought a tricycle was the best approach was Ariel. A pioneer of the British industry, Ariel was one of the many bicycle producing companies which naturally evolved into motorbike manufacturing concerns.

Ariel's tricycle appeared on the market in 1898. Produced at their factory in the Selly Oak district of highly industrialized Birmingham, the tricycle featured an engine made by DeDion in France. The use of French, Belgian, and Swiss engines was a common practice in England then, since few British engines were available in those early days.

The reason why Ariel chose the tricycle approach is not very clear, but the instability of the early motorized bicycles may have been the most important reason. With no method of disengaging the engine from the rear wheel, the motorbikes could topple over quite easily at slow speeds when the motor stopped running, which was a common occurence then with the first primitive carburetors.

The single-cylinder DeDion engine was of the four-stroke type with an overhead intake valve and a side exhaust valve. The exhaust valve was opened by a cam, but the intake valve was pulled open merely by the suction of the piston on its down stroke. On the compression stroke the valve was closed by a weak coil spring on the valve plus the compression pressure in the cylinder.

The lubrication system was the gravity feed type with a small hand lever to control the amount of oil to the engine. The instruction manual advised giving the engine maximum oil when traveling uphill and minimum oil when traveling downhill.

The carburetor was really little more than an evaporator and required the use of a benzine fuel, which evaporates rapidly. A hand lever controlled the amount of benzine that was fed to the engine.

The ignition system consisted of three dry cells and a coil, which was notoriously unreliable in those days. Indeed, the operation of the tricycle was a demanding chore which required considerable dedication to master. A lever had to be used to retard the ignition for starting, and this plus a correct setting of the throttle and compression release were required before the motor would spring into life.

The engine drove the rear axle via a small gear on the crankshaft and a large gear on the rear axle. A large band-type brake was fitted to a band on the gear wheel, which was also operated by a small hand lever.

The fuel tank was of a triangular shape beneath the seat and held about two gallons, while the oil tank was of a cylindrical shape and held about two and one-half gallons.

The DeDion engine had an aluminum alloy crankcase and cast-iron cylinder and

1898 Ariel 500cc Motor Tricycle

stone roads of Birmingham was decidedly rough.

Ariel produced the tricycle until 1903, at which time they dropped the trike and began producing a more orthodox 2-1/2 HP motorbike. The tricycle did not seem to be of an outstanding design, but in 1900 the company did enter one in a 100 mile trial where it beat all of the automobiles in a hill climb and won a first class award.

The Ariel Motor Tricycle is thus a superb example of an early day motorcycle. The few that exist today are highly treasured antiques and always draw a crowd whenever they are exhibited at British vintage bike rallies.

head. The power output was rated at 2.25 HP at around 1000 to 1500 rpm. The top speed of the tricycle was not listed by the factory in their sales brochure, but was probably about 20 to 25 mph, perhaps less.

The tires were the narrow 2-1/2 x 26 inch size in common use in England then, and the outside width of the trike was 42 inches. There was no provision for any suspension system on either the front fork or rear axle, so the ride over the cobble-

Technical Specifications

Engine:	DeDion single cylinder, inlet-over-exhaust-valve type. Surface evaporative carburetor. Battery and coil iginition, hand advance. 2-1/2 HP.
Chassis:	Tubular tricycle frame, rigid. Blade type front fork, rigid.
Transmission:	Direct gear drive to rear axle. Ratio 4.46 to 1. Bicycle pedals for starting.
Tires:	2.25 x 26 inch front and rear.
Brakes:	External band type on a drum on encased gear wheel.
Fuel Tank:	2.0 gallons, triangular type.
Speed:	Estimated 20 to 25 mph.

1905 Indian 253cc 1-3/4 HP
America

By 1905 THE MOTORCYCLE had made some subtle progress. The engine by then was universally mounted in the center of the frame, where its low center of gravity provided a much better handling machine than many of the earlier motorbikes which had their engines mounted higher on the frame. The bicycle type frames were also a bit stronger than the earliest machines, but still very spindly by contemporary standards.

One of the best motorbikes in the world then was Indian. In 1905 Indian sold 1181 motorcycles, one of which was the 1-3/4 HP model shown here. Produced at the Springfield, Massachusetts factory, this machine is an excellent example of the state of the art then.

The 1905 model saw the first improvements made to Oscar Hedstrom's original design of 1901 when a two-way grip was installed on the left handlebar to control both the spark advance as well as the throttle via a set of rods and joints. A new front fork was also used that had a small spring to help dampen the shocks from rough roads.

The engines were produced by the Aurora Company in Illinois, but in 1905 Indian had Aurora produce their engines with a cylinder machined from a solid piece of steel. The single-cylinder engine had a bore and stroke of 2-9/16 x 3.0 inches (65 x 75mm), which provided 15.44 cubic inches or 253cc. A mechanically operated side valve was used for the exhaust, but the intake valve was placed in the head and operated merely by the piston travel plus a weak coil spring. Indian stayed with the IOE design until 1916, but in 1907 they did begin to manufacture their own engines at their Springfield plant.

Despite having a centrally mounted engine, the chassis was little more than a beefed-up bicycle frame. Pedals were fitted for starting the engine and to help the little powerplant pull up a hill. There was no method of disengaging the engine from the rear wheel, since clutches were unheard of then. To start the motorbike the rider first turned on the fuel, then the ignition switch from the batteries, set the spark lever to retard the ignition point, and then pedaled off. To stop the bike the rider shut off the throttle and used the brake — killing the engine every time he stopped.

These early day motorbikes were short and light. The Indian single had a 48 inch wheelbase and weighed only 98 pounds. A bicycle-type New Departure coaster brake was fitted to the rear hub, which was operated by simply reversing the pedal direction. The fuel tank was a slab-type that held about two gallons and was mounted over the rear fender, while the lubrication system was the simple gravity feed type to the engine, which had roller and ball bearings on the rod and crankshaft.

Other than a reliability advantage over most of the other American machines then, the most remarkable thing about these early Indians was the use of chain drive. Indian pioneered this concept right from their beginning, and even won the

1905 Indian 253cc 1-3/4 HP

first three places in the 1911 Isle of Man TT race when their two-speed twins showed the British why a gearbox and chain drive was so superior to the popular single speed, belt drive models.

These early Indians weren't very fast, since the engine was limited to its 1-3/4 rated horsepower at around 2000 rpm by the intake valve, which tended to flutter at higher engine speeds. No speedometers were fitted then, but a 20 to 25 mph speed was probably "flat out." The compression ratio was only about 4.0 to 1 on the Aurora engine, which was kept quite low to suit the poor quality of fuel available then.

Other limiting factors were the poor dry cell ignition batteries in use then and the early carburetors, which flooded easily and thus required a draining and drying out of the carburetor and cylinder before the beast would run again. These two problems were to be overcome within a few years, though, since Indian adopted the Bosch magneto from Germany in 1908 and a new jet-type carburetor a few years later that metered the fuel and provided much cleaner carburetion. A clutch was also added in 1910, which provided much greater versatility, but that is another chapter.

Technical Specifications

Engine:	Thor single cylinder, inlet-over-exhaust-valve type. Solid steel cylinder and head. Bore and stroke 2-9/16 x 3.0 inches, 15.44 cubic inches (253cc). Roller bearing rod. Compression ratio 4.0 to 1. Coil ignition with three dry cells. 1-3/4 HP at about 2000 rpm.
Chassis:	Tubular bicycle type frame, rigid. Cartridge type front fork with small coil spring.
Transmission:	Primary and secondary chains, direct drive. Ratio 8.0 to 1. Bicycle pedals for starting.
Tires:	2.25 x 26 inches front and rear.
Brakes:	New Departure coaster type in rear hub.
Fuel tank:	2.0 gallons, slab type over rear fender.
Dimensions:	Wheelbase 48 inches. Weight 98 pounds.
Speed:	Estimated 20 to 25 mph.

1910 BSA 500cc 4-1/2 HP
England

THE INABILITY to disengage the engine from the rear wheel was a serious limitation to motorcycle controllability in the early days, which prompted nearly all manufacturers to design some type of clutch action in the 1907 to 1910 era. First came the idler devices on belt drive models that simply tightened up the belt, followed by the first true clutch equipped models in 1910.

One of those who adopted a clutch was the Birmingham Small Arms Company in England. An old company formed in 1861 to produce guns, BSA began producing bicycles in 1880. This was followed by the manufacturing of parts for motorcycle producing companies in the early 1900s, which was then followed by the first BSA motorcycle in 1910. The company then steadily grew in stature until, in 1954, they advertised that "one of every four motorcycles sold in the world is a BSA."

The first BSA was a well designed single-cylinder model that featured a side-valve engine — a design that was coming into common use then in England. Both valves were operated by cams, and the valvesprings were lift exposed. Spring breakage was common then due to the poor quality of the steels, and the exposed springs allowed an easy replacement.

With an increased knowledge of cam design plus an improved jet-type carburetor and a Bosch magneto from Germany, the designers were getting more engine speed and power. The 500cc BSA, for instance, turned over at 3000 rpm and developed 3-1/2 HP, with a faster 4-1/2 HP model available.

The 500cc engine had a bore and stroke of 85 x 88mm, and these measurements were destined to remain in use until the last of the illustrious Gold Star models were produced in 1963. The alloy crankcase was fitted with a built-up flywheel that had a roller bearing rod and ball bearing mains, which were fed oil by gravity and a small hand pump. The total-loss lubrication system was the only one known then, with the "used" oil being dumped on the road. A muffler was fitted to silence the exhaust note, but a "cut-out" was fitted that allowed more power and noise when needed — a common practice then.

The new BSA was offered with either a direct belt drive or with a double-cone clutch in the rear hub. The clutch was operated by a lever on the handlebar. In 1911 BSA came out with a two-speed model, with the tiny gearbox also housed in the rear hub. The two-speed model had gear ratios of 5.7 and 7.6 to 1, which gave it the same 30 to 35 mph top speed of the single speeder plus a lower gear for starting and climbing hills. BSA followed this up with a three speed model with chain drive in 1914 that used a countershaft gearbox and clutch — a concept proven by Indian in the 1911 TT.

By 1910 the better motorcycles were a great deal more rugged than the earlier motorbikes. The BSA, for instance, weighed 195 pounds and had a long 56 inch wheelbase. The frame was much stronger, and the cantilever front fork had

1910 BSA 500cc 4-1/2 HP

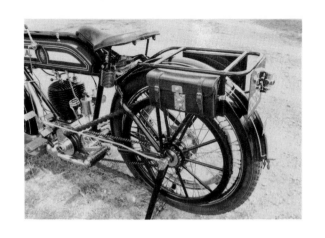

als were fitted for starting the BSA, but a few years later these were dropped when kickstarters were fitted along with a caliper front brake in 1916.

Perhaps the most significant thing about the BSA was the clutch that made the bike so much more controllable and ver-

satile, but equally important was the reliable side-valve engine. Rather oddly, America was to copy this design a few years later and then keep it on the race tracks until 1970 — even though it became obsolete in England by the early 1920s!

a pair of springs to provide an inch or two of travel.

The 1910 BSA and other motorcycles had, by then, adopted a basic design that was true motorcycle and no longer a motorized bicycle. The fuel tank held 2-1/2 gallons and was mounted between the top frame tubes, with a two-quart oil tank contained on the right side. The oil pump was near the front of the tank and was given a few pumps by hand every mile. Only one caliper brake was fitted, and this worked on its own rim on the rear wheel. The tires were the vintage 2-1/2 x 26 inch size, and the handlebar was the vintage pull-back style.

Motorcycles were making some real progress then with lighting sets available as an option that allowed nighttime use. Electric lights were unheard of, so the rider was forced to strike a match to both the front and rear carbide gas lights. Ped-

Technical Specifications

Engine:	Single cylinder, side valve. Bore and stroke 85 x 88mm, 500cc. Cast-iron cylinder and head. Roller bearing rod. Compression ratio 5.0 to 1. Bosch magneto ignition, hand advance. Jet-type carburetor. 3-1/2 or 4-1/2 HP at 3000 rpm.
Chassis:	Tubular, single loop frame, rigid. Cantilever front fork.
Transmission:	Direct belt drive. Double cone clutch in rear hub. Ratio 5.7 to 1.
Tires:	2-1/2 x 26 inch front and rear.
Brakes:	Caliper type on rear rim.
Fuel tank:	2-1/2 gallons.
Dimensions:	Wheelbase 56 inches. Weight 195 pounds.
Speed:	Estimated 30 to 35 mph.

1913 Thor 625cc Model 13-W
America

IN 1911 THERE WERE over 100 makes of motorcycles being produced in America. By 1913 the figure was down to 40, and by 1920 just a handful remained. Those were the sorting-out years in the American industry, with all of the backyard inventors and most of the inferior designs being weeded out in the rough and tumble marketplace.

One of those left on the sidelines by 1920 was Thor. Produced in Aurora, Illinois by the company that manufactured America's first motorcycle engines, Thor first staked out its claim to fame by supplying Indian with their engines until 1907. Thor began manufacturing their own motorcycle in 1903 and continued to produce motorbikes until 1916, at which time they halted production.

The beautiful Thor shown here is a 1913 single that is an excellent example of the American machines of that period. Durable, tough, and fast, it was as good as anything going then and better than most.

Thor offered three models in 1913 — a 61 cubic inch (1000cc) V-twin of 7 HP, a 38-1/8 inch (625cc) 5 HP single, and a 30.5 inch (500cc) 4 HP single. The big twin had a 3.25 x 3.60 inch bore and stroke, as did the 30 inch thumper, while the larger single had 3.5 x 3.80 inch measurements. All engines had an overhead intake valve and side exhaust valve — both operated by cams.

The old and unreliable dry cell-and-coil ignition system had been dropped by then in favor of a Bosch magneto, while the carburetor was a jet type with a "butterfly" valve. Thor also had a mechanical oil pump to push the oil into the engine, which was a much better proposition than the earlier drip-feed systems which relied solely on gravity.

The frame was quite strong and contained a cradle for the engine, which provided a stiffer mount for the powerplant and helped reduce frame flexing. The truss-type front fork contained several small springs, while the tire size was 2-3/4 x 29 inches. A coaster-type brake was fitted to the rear hub, with the wheelbase being rather long at 58 inches.

In line with the trend sweeping America then, Thor used a chain drive, which went directly from the engine to the rear wheel. In order to disengage the engine from the wheel, Thor provided a disc clutch, which was mounted on the end of the crankshaft. Called a "free engine clutch," this handy device was operated by a long handle on the left side of the fuel tank.

Thor also offered a two-speed rear hub then, plus the choice of alternate gear ratios in top gear of 3.70, 3.96, or 4.22 to 1 on the big twin. If the purchaser desired speed for open level roads he selected the 3.70 ratio, but if he had to contend with steep hills the 4.22 ratio was the better choice. The standard ratio for the 38 inch single was 5.0 to 1, and 5.5 to 1 for the 30 inch thumper.

With the fastest ratio the sales brochure claimed the big twin would run 60 to 65 mph, while the singles were capable of 30 to 35 mph. With the cast-iron pistons in use then the engine could turn up to only about 2500 rpm with safety — anything more than this invited piston seizure.

1913 Thor 625cc Model 13-W

With a weight of 225 pounds in twin-cylinder form and 190 in single-cylinder guise, these Thors were durable machines with an excellent reputation. By 1913 the company was considered to be one of the top five makes in America, along with Indian, Harley-Davidson, Excelsior, and Merkel, but sales never did come close to what Harley and Indian achieved.

Finished in either white or blue and with some nickel plating (chrome wasn't used then), the 1913 Thor was a handsome machine. The sweptback handlebar and 2-3/4 gallon fuel tank had a proper vintage look, as did the tall and narrow wheels and skinny little fenders. A one gallon oil tank was also contained in the top tank section, while a tool box was mounted beneath the seat.

With its bicycle pedals for starting and its bicycle-type seat, the Thor 13-W is a superb example of what a good motorcycle looked like in those final days just before World War I. The Thor did not see the light of day after the war, however, and one more beautiful machine was thus relegated to the history books.

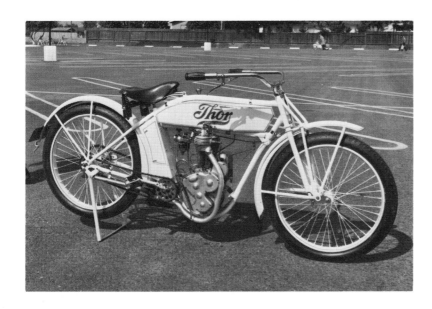

Technical Specifications

Engine:	Single cylinder, inlet-over-exhaust-value type. Bore and stroke 3.57 x 3.80 inches, 38-1/8 cubic inches (625cc). Roller bearing rod. Compression ratio 4.5 to 1. Bosch magneto ignition, hand advance. Thor butterfly valve carburetor. 5 HP at about 2500 rpm.
Chassis:	Tubular, cradle type frame, rigid. Thor truss front fork with springs.
Transmission:	Direct chain drive, single speed with clutch on engine shaft. Two speed rear hub optional. Ratio 5.0 to 1. Bicycle pedals for starting.
Tires:	2-3/4 x 29 inch front and rear.
Brakes:	Thor coaster disc type in rear hub.
Fuel tank:	2-3/4 gallons.
Dimensions:	Wheelbase 58 inches. Weight 190 pounds.
Speed:	About 30-35 mph.

1916 Indian 500cc Model H
America

DIRT AND BOARD track racing was a great spectacle in the early days of American motorcycle sport. Huge crowds flocked to see the fire-belching beasts perform, and great advertising advantages were gained with each great win.

In such an environment Indian was naturally in the thick of things. They were a world leader then, and their engineering was brilliant.

In 1908 the company fielded their first racing models, followed in 1911 by a radically new overhead valve design in which four valves were used per cylinder. The idea behind the four valves was not so much a gain in power, but rather to overcome the problem of valve breakage. Racing engines run very hot, and the valve steels available then wouldn't stand up to this heat without breaking. A smaller valve can better disipate its heat into the head and thus run cooler, which is exactly what Indian was seeking in its unique 4-valve design.

The new 4-valve 500cc single and 8-valve 1000cc V-twin proved to be a smashing success. Of a parallel valve design (the hemispherical head had yet to be invented), the new design also proved to be a great deal faster after Indian learned to pep up the valve timing to take advantage of the increased valve area and capacity for greater revs.

In 1916 Indian decided to produce these racers for sale to the public. In the following years they sold a modest number — a few of which still exist as American classics of incomparable stature. The 1916 Indian racer shown here, which has some non-authentic parts, is one of those classics.

The Model H racer had a bore and stroke of 3-1/8 x 3-31/32 inches. No power output was listed by the factory, but 35 HP at around 5000 rpm has been estimated by authorities for the 500cc single and 50 HP for the 61 inch twin. Indian fitted their own carburetor to the bikes and used very short exhaust pipes, while a gear pump fed oil to the engine. A hand pump was also fitted for use when really "flat out."

To transmit the power, Indian used a primary chain, a countershaft with multiplate clutch, and a rear chain. No gearbox was needed on the one-half or one-mile dirt tracks or the big board tracks, so it was dispensed with to save some weight.

The frame was made of chromevanadium steel tubing for toughness, which had a rigid truss-type front fork. The 2.25 x 28 inch tires were pumped up to nearly 100 pounds, which combined with the lack of any suspension to provide a bone-jarring ride. Pedals were provided for starting, but these and the rear stand and footpegs were discarded by most riders for the ultimate in a tucked-in riding position.

The carburetor was set up to be all on or all off. A kill button was used to cut the power for the corners, which resulted in a wild riding style. On dirt tracks the rider had to learn to control a power slide or fall off! Only one brake was fitted, since the big tracks required speed, not stopping!

With its bright red paint scheme with gold striping, tall wheels, and dropped

1916 Indian 500cc Model H

handlebar, the racer was a sight to make the pulse pound. Intended for the Class A formula in use then, the racers burned alcohol fuels and went like hell. Lap speeds of over 100 mph became common, with 85 mph averages being chalked up by the big twins in long distance races of 100, 200, and even 300 miles.

Under the rules then, most of the professional races were for 61 inch motors, with the 500cc single intended mainly for the amateur riders. The singles were used on the dirt tracks by the professional riders in selected races, however, with track records for one mile dirt tracks being set in the 78 to 81 mph range.

Indian continued to develop their 4-valve design until it was capable of incredible speeds. In 1926 Johnny Seymour set a new American 500cc speed record of 115.64 mph over the sands of Daytona Beach, Florida, which was well beyond anything clocked in Europe by 30 inch motors and not far shy of the F.I.M. world speed record of 121.41 mph set by a British 1000cc V-twin. Running on a tall 4.4 to 1 gear ratio, Seymour's Indian would have been turning over at 6700 rpm — an incredible engine speed for those days.

By then the golden years of motorcycle sport were coming to an end in America, however, since the people had aban-

doned their bikes to enjoy the comfort of a car. Sales tumbled, and the factories soon found they could no longer afford exotic racing machines and a big team of highly paid factory riders backed up with designers and mechanics. In 1933 the Class A racers were phased out in favor of less sophisticated designs, and the great Indian 4-valvers became just a legend of the past.

Technical Specifications

Engine:	Single cylinder, 4 valve overhead valve. Bore and stroke 3-1/8 x 3-31/32 inches, 30.5 cubic inches (500cc). Cast-iron cylinder and head. Roller bearing rod. Compression ratio 7 to 1 up to 9 to 1. Dixie magneto. Estimated 35 HP at 5000 rpm.
Chassis:	Single loop, tubular frame, rigid. Indian truss fork, rigid.
Transmission:	Primary and secondary chains, countershaft with clutch. Gear ratios to suit the track.
Tires:	2.25 x 28 inch front and rear.
Brakes:	External band type on rear wheel, back-pedal control.
Fuel tank:	Various sizes available, 2-1/2 gallon standard.
Dimensions:	Wheelbase 53 inches. Weight about 190 pounds.
Speed:	80 to 86 mph, depending upon state of tune.

1916 Harley-Davidson 1000cc Model 11
America

WORLD WAR I gave a great boost to the Harley-Davidson Motor Company. Spurred on by military orders that totaled over 20,000 machines, H-D prospered and grew as never before.

Perhaps the most significant thing about the 1914 to 1917 war was the requirement that the military motorcycles be tough, durable, and perform in an effective manner. This requirement motivated Harley to push a little harder to make their machines more modern, which resulted in their first chain drive model in 1913 and a new two-speed model in 1914. The 1914 Harleys also had a kickstarter, floorboards, and an internal expanding band rear brake, with the new gears being located in the rear hub.

In 1915 the Milwaukee, Wisconsin concern became really modern when they introduced new single and twin-cylinder models with a three-speed countershaft gearbox and clutch. This enabled the Harleys to negotiate very steep hills and poor roads — something the earlier models had been reluctant to do.

Other improvements in 1915 included a new mechanical oil pump to replace the earlier gravity-feed system, which provided improved lubrication to the engine and thus allowed the designers to extract more power from the engines. Faster cams, larger valves, improved porting, a larger carburetor, and heavier flywheels were used, which pushed the revs up to 3000 rpm from 2500 revs for 6 HP from the 35 inch single and 11 HP on the big 61 inch twin.

Another great improvement in 1915 was the use of electric lights on the 17-J Model. A magneto was used for ignition, but a generator and battery provided convenient lighting for night-time use.

Harley-Davidson was engaged in a heated sales battle then with Indian, which motivated them to produce even faster models for 1917. The 35 inch single, which had a 3-5/16 x 4.0 inch bore and stroke for 565cc, was continued at 6 HP, but the new 1000cc "Master Motor" pumped out a solid 16 HP and ran over 60 mph.

Harley produced both single-speed and three-speed models that year, with the single speeders having a countershaft clutch and lower selling price. More braking power was needed to control this wild outburst of speed, which motivated the designers to use a new binder with both internal and external brake bands. The "service" brake for regular use was operated by a foot pedal on the right floorboard and was mounted inside of the drum, while a hand lever on the right handlebar operated the "auxiliary" brake on the outside of the same drum. The auxiliary binder was called into use when descending steep hills or for panic stops.

The exhaust system contained a proper muffler and a "cut-out," which was operated by a left-side foot lever. The use of the cut-out provided an open exhaust system with more power and lots of noise, which the young bloods loved to use for climbing steep hills out in the "boonies."

Another big improvement was the Schebler carburetor, which was fitted with a choke to aid in starting a motor when

1916 Harley-Davidson 1000cc Model 11

cold. The throttle was controlled from the left twistgrip, which was a two-way affair to also control the spark retard mechanism for starting.

The manufacturers were paying greater attention then to rider comfort. The H-D front fork was a good one for those days and featured two trailing links from the front axle to the main fork tubes. These links swiveled on the fork legs and worked against long tubes which contained a pair of long springs for compression and two shorter springs for rebound damping. The springs allowed about two inches of travel. Not to be content with their outstanding fork, Harley also fitted a full floating seat which had the normal pair of coil springs plus a long telescopic coil spring in the frame tube. This was real progress and a boon over rough roads. Greater weather protection was also provided by the 5-1/4 inch wide fenders, which made the Harley much more substantial looking than the earlier models.

One other interesting feature of this era was the popularity of the sidecar. Harley produced both passenger sidecars and commercial vans then, as did a host of proprietary manufacturers. Many sidecars were sold then, and today they are the center of attraction at any vintage motorcycle rally.

Technical Specifications

Engine: Twin cylinder, inlet-over-exhaust-valve type. Bore and stroke 3-5/16 x 3-1/2 inches, 61 cubic inches (1000cc). Cast-iron cylinders and heads. Roller bearing rods. Schebler carburetor. Magneto ignition or Remy generator and coil ignition. 11 HP at 3000 rpm.

Chassis: Single loop, tubular frame, rigid. Trailing link front fork.

Transmission: Primary and secondary chains. Hand shift. Ratios 3.89, 5.83, and 8.75 to 1.

Tires: 3.00 x 28 inch front and rear.

Brakes: 7/8 x 7-5/16 inch rear drum, external and internal bands.

Fuel tank: 2-3/4 gallons with 5-1/2 pint auxiliary tank.

Dimensions: Wheelbase 59-1/2 inches. Weight 250 pounds.

Speed: 60 mph.

1928 BMW 750cc R62

Germany

THE BMW HAS LONG been regarded as the world's finest motorcycle. Never one to place sheer speed before a smooth performance, the twins from Munich have always been known for their smooth engines and ability to run for very long mileages with little maintenance.

Often called the "Rolls-Royce of motorcycles," the BMW was first produced in 1923. The first BMW was a 500cc opposed twin with shaft drive and a unit construction of the engine and gearbox, which set the mold that all twin-cylinder BMWs were to follow forever after. Only a few vertical singles of 400cc size or smaller would ever violate this principle.

The advantages of the BMW design were several. The first was the lack of engine vibrations due to the two pistons balancing each other out so perfectly, and the second was the superior cooling of the two cylinders which stick out in the air stream so well. Still another was the low center of gravity that enhanced the handling, and yet another advantage was the accessibility for maintenance.

The first side-valve BMW was followed in 1925 by two overhead valve models — a 250cc single and a 500cc twin. All of these early BMWs were equipped with an internal expanding front brake — an innovative feature for those days. The 16 HP twin still had a caliper brake on a rear rim, however, plus the hand shifter for the three-speed gearbox.

In 1926 the rear brake was changed to the internal expanding type, and then in 1928 the company produced larger 750cc models in both side-valve and overhead valve variations. The flathead model churned out 18 HP at 3400 rpm, while the OHV version developed 24 HP at 4000 rpm. The OHV model was successfully supercharged a few years later and set a new world speed record of 137.58 mph in 1930, and then on up to 159.01 mph in 1935 — achievements that helped get the name better known outside of Germany.

The BMW shown here is a 1928 R62 side valver with the big 750cc engine that was so suitable for sidecar use. Not as fast as the OHV model, the R62 had gobs of torque low down in the rev range where it was needed for pulling a sidecar.

The large alloy crankcase held the oil reservoir, with the oil being returned to the tank after it had passed through the engine. These circulating lubrication systems first came into use in Europe in the early 1920s and were a big improvement over the earlier total-loss systems in which the "used" oil was dumped onto the road. Solid progress.

The R62 still had the vintage fuel tank between the top frame tubes, since the "saddle" tank had just been invented in England. It did have modern 19 inch wheels and a leaf-spring front fork, however, which helped smooth out the roads and thus provide a wee bit more comfort than the earlier narrow-tire models. Lights were still optional then on most of the world's motorcycles, since the roads of the world were still mostly dirt and rough — not the best for riding at night.

Despite not being sold in any numbers outside of Germany, the BMW was surely

1928 BMW 750cc R62

one of the world's outstanding machines then. Its reliability would be good even today, since the Bosch magneto and new lubrication system were both first class. England by then was producing a greater variety of motorcycles, especially for sporting use, but the 1928 BMWs certainly proved that the motorcycle was coming of age. The chain that jerked, the oil being dumped onto the road, the exposed valve gear that leaked oil all over the engine, the hard starting, and the general lack of reliability — these were all a thing of the past with the new BMW. Smooth, clean, and reliable, the motorcycle had at last arrived as a truly acceptable form of transportation.

The only problem facing BMW was that few people outside of Germany had ever heard of the marque, let alone knew what a superior machine it was. The only answer was to go racing, which was the best way to gain acceptance then in the international market. By then the value of racing publicity had greatly diminished in America, but in Europe the grand prix scene was developing into a tremendous spectacle.

BMW began playing around with superchargers in the late 1920s on their speed record models, but it was not until Otto Ley and Karl Gall swept to victory in the 1936 Swedish Grand Prix that Europe

began to really take notice. In 1937, Jock West, Ley, and Gall won four of the nine grand prix events, and then in 1938 the great Georg Meier won the European 500cc championship to bring BMW nearly unlimited prestige and fame. Meier and West then finished 1-2 in the 1939 Senior TT before the war halted all motorcycle sports.

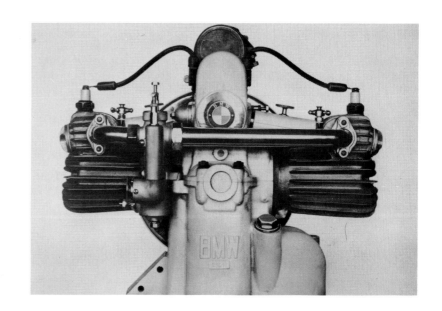

Technical Specifications

Engine:	Opposed twin cylinder, side valve. Bore and stroke 78 x 78mm, 745cc. Cast-iron cylinders with alloy heads. Roller bearing rods. Compression ratio 5.5 to 1. Two BMW 28mm carburetors. Bosch magneto ignition. 18 HP at 3400 rpm.
Chassis:	Twin loop cradle frame, rigid. Leaf spring front fork.
Transmission:	Shaft drive, geared primary. Hand shift. Ratios 4.05, 6.30, and 11.5 to 1. Sidecar 4.75 to 1 top gear.
Tires:	3.25 x 19 inch front, 3.50 x 19 inch rear.
Brakes:	1.0 x 7.0 inches, drum type.
Fuel tank:	3.1 gallons.
Dimensions:	Wheelbase 55.0 inches. Weight 341 pounds.
Speed:	71 mph.

1929 Cleveland 1000cc 4-61
America

ONE OF THE MOST colorful legends in American motorcycle history is the story of the great four-cylinder machines. Intended to be sophisticated, fast, smooth, and expensive, the great American fours were a prestigious mount for the discriminating owner who was willing to pay a premium for the finest motorcycle in the world.

Pierce started America's four-cylinder story in 1909 after studying the design of the 1904 FN from Belgium. The Pierce was followed by the Henderson in 1912 and the Ace in 1920. Indian then purchased the Ace Company in 1927, after which they marketed their illustrious four until early in 1942 when the last of America's fours were produced.

There was, however, one other American four, which was produced by the Cleveland Motorcycle Company in Cleveland, Ohio. First produced in 1925 as a 670cc OHV model with a camshaft on each side of the crankshaft, the Cleveland four was punched out to 750cc in 1926

and changed to the IOE or "F head" type as it is known in America.

The Cleveland wasn't fast enough to keep up with the huge 74 to 80 inch Harleys, Hendersons, Aces, and Indians, though, so the 75 mph 45 incher was dropped in favor of a larger 61 cubic inch model in 1927 that would run 90 mph.

As was common to all American fours, the 4-61 model had its engine in line with the frame and was of the F head design. The cylinders were cast in one block, as was the head. A Bosch magneto was used for ignition, while a generator and battery fed the lights, which were standard equipment by then on American machines.

In contrast to most of the European in-line fours that used shaft drive, nearly all of the American fours used a right-angle gearbox and chain drive. A wide twin-tube frame was used to house the massive engine, along with a unique trailing-link front fork which had a large coil spring mounted in a cylinder just in front of the steering head. Another innovative idea

was the front brake — a really progressive concept then in America. A side stand was also fitted, which was one of the first uses of this handy device.

Never one to sit on their laurels, Cleveland produced an even faster model in 1929. Called the Tornado, this 1000cc model had Dow metal pistons, which were one ounce lighter than aluminum pistons, a higher compression ratio, larger valves, and larger intake ports. Fitted with a new frame which lowered the seating position 2-1/2 inches plus a new sloping fuel tank, the Tornado looked fast while sitting still. The top speed was 100 mph, which was very quick then.

An even faster model was produced in 1930 called the Century, which had enlarged and polished ports, an even higher compression ratio, a special exhaust system, and a triple-spring front fork. Every Century model was tested by the factory before being offered for sale to ensure that it would clock 100 mph, after which a small brass tag was riveted to one of the intake valve covers.

1929 Cleveland 1000cc 4-61

The new Cleveland was an expensive machine to produce, however, and with the stock market crash in October of 1929 came the start of the terrible depression. Business worsened rapidly in 1930, and sales fell drastically. The company was soon bankrupt after having produced just a small number of Century models, so that the luxurious Cleveland passed quietly from the scene.

Altogether about 40,000 Cleveland fours were produced from 1925 to early 1930. The 1929 4-61 model shown here is one of those bikes. Beautifully restored, it well represents the line of thought used in all American four-cylinder models from 1909 to 1942 when the last Indians were built.

The basic design was massive and yielded a long and heavy machine that was rather clumsy about town but a joy on the open road where it was serene, stable, and smooth as silk. The big V-twins of those days tended to shake the rider to pieces with their vibration, so the smooth power delivery of the four was sweet and silky by comparison.

These old fours were slow revvers compared to the high revving fours we know today, since their long strokes and limited breathing ability just didn't allow lots of revs. The long strokes provided gobs of torque low down in the rev range,

however, so that the power delivery was smooth from zero revs on up. The flexibility of the engine was exceptional, and they were a very relaxing machine to ride.

The economic crash of the 1930s was not the place to be selling expensive

four-cylinder motorcycles, however, so that only the Indian was to survive. The beautiful blue Cleveland thus quietly passed from the scene, only to be resurrected many years later and restored to all of its former glory. Elegant and with the four-cylinder drone, the Cleveland well represents the romantic era of American four-cylinder motorcycles.

Technical Specifications

Engine:	Four cylinder, F head. 61 cubic inches, 1000cc. Cast-iron cylinder and head. Plain bearing rods. Compression ratio 6.0 to 1. Linkert 1-1/4 inch carburetor. Bosch magneto ignition. Estimated 28 HP at 4500 rpm.
Chassis:	Twin loop cradle frame, rigid. Trailing link front fork.
Transmission:	Geared primary, secondary chain. Hand shift. Ratios 3.80, 5.83, and 9.98 to 1.
Tires:	4.00 x 19 inch front and rear.
Brakes:	1.0 x 6.0 inches, drum type.
Fuel tank:	4.5 gallons.
Dimensions:	Wheelbase 61 inches. Weight 540 pounds.
Speed:	90 mph.

1933 Velocette 350cc KTT
England

FOR PURE HISTORIC significance, it would be hard to beat the story of the KTT Velocette. In 1926 the company became the first to win a TT race with an overhead camshaft engine. In 1928 Velocette invented the positive-stop foot gearshift, and then in 1929 they became the first to offer a replica road racer for sale to the public. In 1936 the works racers were the first to appear with a modern swinging-arm rear suspension, which was followed by the first sale of this design on their 1939 KTT replica road racing model.

The overhead camshaft engine is what the marque is most famous for, which was widely copied by others after Canadian Alec Bennett won the 1926 Junior TT at the record speed of 66.70 mph. Velocettes won again in 1928 and 1929, which prompted them to produce a KTT model in 1929 for sale to the private owners. Up to that time the poor privateers were forced to modify standard roadsters, which were too slow and unreliable to stay up with the "works" racing machines. The first 348cc KTT engine had a 7.5 to

1 compression ratio and ran about 85 mph on 50-50 petrol-benzol fuel. The 1-1/16 inch carburetor breathed into a deep hemispherical combustion chamber, with two pairs of bevel gears and a vertical shaft driving the single overhead camshaft. The engine turned over at up to 6000 rpm and worked through a three-speed gearbox with ratios of 5.25, 7.6, and 9.94 to 1. Weighing only 265 pounds, the KTT went like a bomb and won races for its riders all over Europe.

The KTT was steadily developed by the factory — first on their works bikes and then incorporating what they had learned on the KTT production model. In 1932 the coil valvesprings were replaced with the new hairpin type, and then in 1933 a new Mk IV model was introduced that featured a four-speed gearbox. Just a few Mk IV models were produced before a change was made from a cast-iron head to a bronze head that ran much cooler and thus allowed an increase in the compression ratio.

The KTT used the circulating oil system

that had been adopted by the British industry in the early 1920s. A BTH racing magneto was fitted, as was a long straight pipe exhaust system. The Mk IV engine developed 25 to 27 HP at 6200 rpm, which propelled it to speeds of 90-95 mph. A 3-1/2 gallon fuel tank was mounted over the top frame tubes in the "saddle" position, with the cylindrical oil tank holding three quarts.

The frame was rigid and had extra braces on the rear end to strengthen things up a bit, while the front fork was the girder type that was coming into universal use then in England. The 21 inch tire size was still favored for road racing then to provide adequate ground clearance when cornering, but the British roadsters were changing over to the 19 inch size. The brakes were husky 7.0 inch units that seemed powerful for those days but would be pitiful today, but then the KTT weighed only 270 pounds on its 53-3/4 inch wheelbase.

With its overhead cam engine, the 350cc single could be revved higher than

1933 Velocette 350cc KTT

a pushrod engine with little fear of valve float, which made the OHC models both faster and more reliable than the OHV models. Following Velocette's great TT wins there was a big switch to the OHC design by other manufacturers — first on their works racers, then their replica racers, and lastly some high performance road models. Velocette was first, though, both with their KTT racer and their KSS roadster, which gave them an enviable place in the market place as well as later in the history books.

The 1933 KTT Mk IV shown here is slightly non-authentic with a tachometer and later style front wheel, but it still well represents why England assumed the world technological lead in the late 1920s with superb engineering in a wide variety of models. The grand prix scene and the marketplace both received a setback in the early 1930s due to the effects of the depression, but by 1935 things were looking up and dozens of factories became involved in the racing game to seek the ultimate in publicity. The grand prix and England had both come of age.

The 1933 KTT also set a new standard for roadability, since the British were beginning to understand what steering geometry, frame designing, and handling were all about. Fast, nearly unburstable,

and with a great feel for the road, the KTT was an engineering masterpiece as well as a work of art.

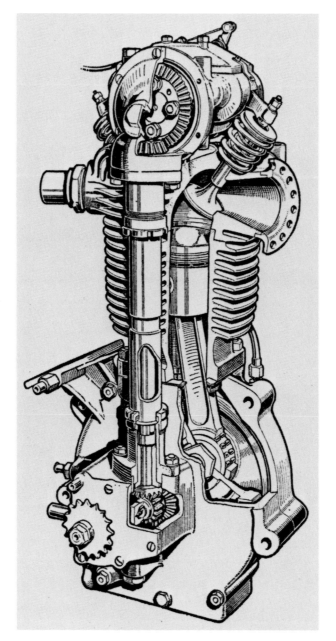

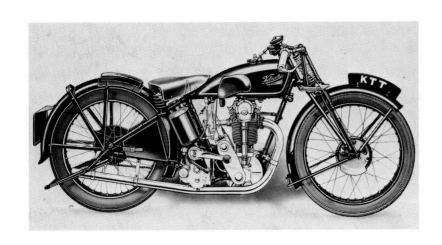

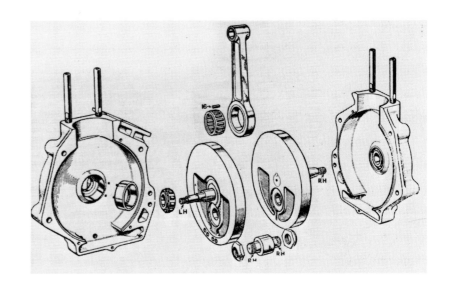

Technical Specifications

Engine:	Single cylinder, overhead camshaft. Bore and stroke 74 x 81mm, 350cc. Cast-iron cylinder and head, bronze head on later models. Roller bearing rod. 7.5 to 1 compression ratio. Amal 1-1/16 inch TT carburetor. BTH racing magneto. 25-27 HP at 6200 rpm.
Chassis:	Single loop frame, rigid. Webb girder front fork.
Transmission:	Primary and secondary chains. Foot shift. Ratios 5.05, 5.55, 7.30, and 9.6 to 1.
Tires:	2.75 x 21 inch front and rear.
Brakes:	1.0 x 7.0 inches, drum type.
Fuel tank:	3-1/2 gallons.
Dimensions:	Wheelbase 53-3/4 inches. Weight 270 pounds.
Speed:	90-95 mph.

1937 Moto Guzzi 500cc GT
Italy

THE YEAR OF 1928 is especially significant in the history of the motorcycle, since this was the year when the spring frame motorcycle finally came of age. Up to that time there had been little real progress in designing a good spring frame, but with the advent of the Moto Guzzi GT and Vincent-HRD, the future of the rear suspension system was assured.

In the early days there had been some notable efforts made at producing an acceptable rear suspension, with the 1909 Merkel and 1913 Indian being produced in America for a few years as was the 1920 Nimbus in Denmark. All of these were dropped in favor of rigid frame models, however, since the riders often complained of poor handling and speed wobbles.

This distrust of spring frames was especially true in Europe, where the widely held theory was that springers hopped around too much to be controllable. The culprit was the lack of hydraulic damping on rebound, since hydraulically dampened shocks had yet to be invented. The

general lack of torsional strength in the light frames also contributed to the bike's tendency to wobble a bit after a bad bump in the road, which had the road racing fraternity convinced that a spring frame racer would be nothing less than lethal for its rider.

All of this began to change in 1928 with the new Guzzi 500cc GT model, which had a well designed frame that didn't flex plus a pivoted-fork rear suspension that was also strong enough to resist bending under load. In the Guzzi design a long triangular fork was used which pivoted at the front on the top tubes. The bottom tubes connected to a pair of coil springs, which were mounted to the frame beneath the engine. The damping action was provided by a pair of friction discs on two scissors-type arms above the rear axle.

The Guzzi idea was brilliant and provided about three inches of travel. The frame didn't flex, and the Gran Turismo model set a new standard in riding comfort.

There was still great skepticism in Europe about spring frames, however, which motivated Guzzi to prove the merits of their design on their works road racing machines. Guzzi had always had a passion for racing since their birth in 1923, which led them to the famous Isle of Man in 1935. The great Stanley Woods was hired to ride their bikes that year, which consisted of a 250cc single and a 500cc V-twin. These Guzzis were unproven outside of Italy, so that few observers gave the twin much chance against the invincible Norton singles in the Senior TT.

Stanley, however, confounded the experts with two great wins — the first ever by spring frame models over the demanding 37-3/4 mile TT course. In the Senior TT Stanley came from 26 seconds behind on lap six to score a last-lap victory over Jimmy Guthrie by four tiny seconds — still the closest Senior TT on record. Stanley also set new lap and race records at 86.53 and 84.68 mph. These convincing wins stunned the racing world and started

1937 Moto Guzzi 500cc GT

a wholesale move to a wide variety of spring frame designs in 1936.

The Guzzi shown here is a 1937 500cc GT model with the original spring frame design that Guzzi retained clear into the 1950s. Slightly non-authentic, this cobby looking thumper has the traditional Guzzi features of a horizontal engine with outside flywheel — features laid down in the first Guzzi and continued until the last of the Falcone models in 1957.

The Guzzi GT had an oversquare engine with a bore and stroke of 88 x 82mm. The engine was rated at 24 HP at 4500 rpm, but this must have been the peak torque speed rather than peak horsepower speed since the single would thump on out to 90 mph where it was turning over at 5500 rpm on its tall gear ratio.

The horizontal engine required the use of a long 59 inch wheelbase, which combined with a girder front fork to provide a stable bike at high speeds. Guzzis have always had good brakes, but the monstrous ten inch front binder on this bike must have been taken from a Condor road racing model to replace the original eight inch unit.

Moto Guzzi thus has a unique place in the history of the motorcycle. The winner of many TTs, grands prix, and world championships after the war and up to

their final year of racing in 1957, the marque should be remembered for their 1935 TT wins when they proved to the world that the spring frame was the only way to go.

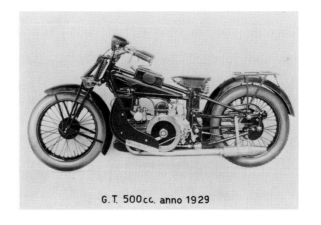

G.T. 500cc. anno 1929

54

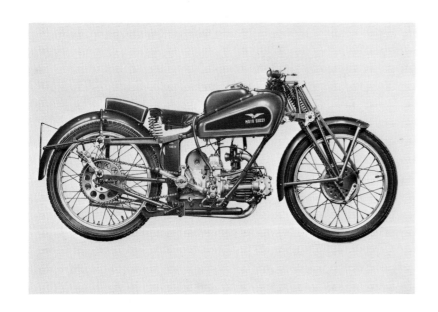

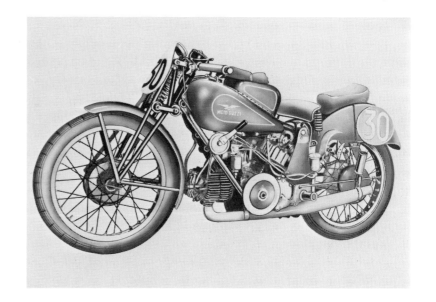

Technical Specifications

Engine:	Horizontal single cylinder, overhead valve. Bore and stroke 88 x 82mm, 500cc. Cast-iron head and cylinder. Roller bearing rod. Compression ratio 6.5 to 1. Del Orto carburetor. Magneto ignition. 24 HP at 4500 rpm.
Chassis:	Twin loop frame, pivoted fork rear suspension. Girder front fork.
Transmission:	Gear primary, secondary chain. Foot shift. Ratios 4.70, 6.19, 8.14, and 10.77 to 1.
Tires:	3.25 x 19 inch front, 3.50 x 19 inch rear.
Brakes:	1.5 x 8.0 inches front, 1.0 x 7.0 inches rear. Drum type.
Fuel tank:	3.0 gallons.
Dimensions:	Wheelbase 59 inches. Weight 380 pounds.
Speed:	90 mph.

1937 Indian 750cc Sport Scout
America

OF ALL THE AMERICAN racing machines, the Indian Sport Scout is probably the most classic. First produced in 1935, the Sport Scout went on to establish a tremendous record in American dirt track events before World War II and again after the war until 1953 when the Indian Company went broke.

The last in a long line of side-valve Indians that stretched back to 1916, the Sport Scout was the very heart and soul of what the new Class C racing formula was all about. First used in 1933 to replace the old Class A formula, Class C rules required the use of standard road model designs which could be modified for racing. Alcohol fuels were no longer allowed, with motors up to 750cc in side-valve form and 500cc in OHV or OHC forms. In addition, the formula allowed no more than a 7.0 to 1 compression ratio — a rule that did not hinder the flatheads but did slow down the OHV models.

The 45 inch Scout had a 42° V-twin engine with cast-iron cylinders and alloy heads. Weighing 436 pounds and with a tall 4.81 gear ratio, a stock Sport Scout would run about 80 mph.

The Scout shown here is a racer and somewhat different than a road model. Restored in 1979 by Indian expert Sammy Pierce, Old Number 38 was made famous by Ed Kretz. Before he retired from racing in 1955, Kretz became a living legend on the dusty dirt tracks of America with wins in such historic races as the 200 mile national championships at Savannah, Georgia in 1936 and Daytona Beach in 1937, the Langhorne 100 mile nationals in 1938, 1939, and 1940, and the 1938 Laconia 200 miler.

After the war Kretz proceeded to win the 1946 Lacomia 100 mile classic, the 1948 Langhorne 100 mile national, the 1948 Riverside 100 mile TT in California, and fourteen Pacific Coast Championships. Ed's last national win was the 1954 100 mile flat track race at historic Carroll Speedway in Los Angeles, after which he retired to polish his 300 trophies.

The most historic win was the 1937 Daytona Beach race, since that was the first motorcycle race ever held at Daytona. Kretz's victory thus started a legacy at this now famous place, which was a combination sand-beach and paved-road course in 1937.

A true works racer supplied by the factory, the 1937 Scout ran on a 6.5 to 1 compression ratio and breathed through a single 1-1/2 inch Linkert carburetor. Fitted with very special cams and a pair of 30 inch long straight pipes, Old Number 38 produced 41 HP at 6500 rpm. Geared 6.50 for one-half mile tracks, Kretz could hit 90 mph on the straights. On the taller 4.74 to 1 ratio for the one-mile tracks he could nudge 105. And with flat-out gearing of 4.33 for Daytona the bike would run 114 mph. Kretz, however, claims that the bike has been clocked at 121 mph at 6900 rpm — an incredible performance for a 1937 side-valve engine!

Set up with brakes and the standard 3.7 gallon fuel tank with a 2-1/2 quart oil compartment, the first Daytona winner weighed in at 360 pounds. Brakes were not allowed then on the flat tracks, how-

1937 Indian 750cc Sport Scout

ever, which dropped the weight to 310 pounds when fitted with a smaller fuel tank.

With a wheelbase of 56 inches and big 4.00 inch tires, the Indian handled to perfection on the smooth dirt tracks. And with a tremendous amount of mid-range punch, the acceleration was also outstanding — the prime ingredients for victory in the dirt.

Despite his excellence on the flat tracks and in dirt track TT-type racing, Kretz was never able to win again at Daytona. This was, perhaps, the subtle difference between Harley-Davidson durability and Indian speed in those days when the rivalry between the two makes was so fierce. This rivalry was jolted in 1941, however, when Billy Mathews came from Canada with his Norton Manx single to trounce all the flatheads at Daytona.

After the war the side-valvers once again proved victorious at Daytona in 1947 and 1948, but in 1949 Mathews and a youngster named Dick Klamfoth ran off four consecutive Norton wins to prove to the Americans that the old side-valve design was really rather ancient. The Americans, however, fought back clear up to 1970 and proved that under a protective formula the flatheads were still a winning design.

Old Number 38 is thus a magnificent classic from that unique era between the depression and the 1950s when America discovered that side-valve engines were obsolete on the international scene. Designed and raced by men who were unconcerned about anything not produced in America, the 1937 Sport Scout is a monument to an engineering ideal that time was destined to doom to antiquity. A true work of art, Old Number 38 is a timeless classic of the side-valve motors that once ruled the dusty dirt tracks of America.

Technical Specifications

Engine:	42° V-twin, side valve. Bore and stroke 2-7/8 x 3-1/2 inches, 45 cubic inches (750cc). Cast-iron cylinders, alloy heads. Roller bearing rods. Compression ratio 6.5 to 1. Linkert 1-1/2 inch carburetor. Bosch or Splitdorf magneto. 41 HP at 6500 rpm.
Chassis:	Single loop, cradle frame, rigid. Girder front fork.
Transmission:	Gear primary, secondary chain. Hand shift, three speed. Ratios — 6.50 for one-half mile track, 4.74 for one mile track, 4.33 for Daytona Beach track.
Tires:	4.00 x 19 inch front, 4.00 x 18 inch rear.
Brakes:	1.5 x 7.0 inches, drum type.
Fuel tank:	3.7 gallons.
Dimensions:	Wheelbase 56 inches. Weight 360 pounds.
Speed:	114 mph on Daytona gearing.

1939 CZ 125cc 125A
Czechoslovakia

WITH THE TERRIBLE depression behind them, many European countries entered into a period of prosperity in the late 1930s that offered some new business opportunities to motorbike manufacturers. One of those who recognized this new market potential was the CZ concern in Strakonice, Czechoslovakia.

Up to the late 1930s the motorcycle had not been sufficiently reliable or manageable to attract anyone but a serious motorcycle enthusiast who had to be somewhat athletic to operate his machine as well as willing to work on the thing to keep it running. By the late 1930s the mechanics of the motorcycle had become reasonably reliable and the bikes so easy to ride that a whole new market was opened up of young people, women, and those not mechanically inclined.

The increasing prosperity then also allowed thousands of Europeans to park their bicycles and purchase motorbikes, which offered a whole new market for the manufacturers. CZ recognized this market potential and designed a small motorcycle

to meet this need. Inexpensive to purchase and maintain and easy to ride, the new CZ was a great success in the marketplace of Eastern Europe.

Called the 125A, the new CZ was the product of a company that dates back to 1919 when their factory turned out guns. Bicycles were added in 1930, which almost immediately acquired a 76cc motor over the front wheel. In 1931 the engine was mounted centrally in the frame, and then came a larger 175cc model in 1935. A 250cc 9 HP model was introduced in 1936, followed by a 500cc twin in 1937.

This twin was quite modern and used the new loop-scavenging design that had been invented by Dr. Schnurle at the DKW works in Germany a few years earlier. This invention at last made the two-stroke a more acceptable competitor to the four-stroke models, since the performance was improved and the spark plug fouling and piston seizure tendencies were greatly reduced.

In an effort to produce an inexpensive and easily ridden lightweight, CZ offered a

98cc motorcycle in 1937 that had a 2.5 HP engine and hand shifted, three-speed gearbox. In early 1939 an improved 125A model was introduced, which had a stronger 4.5 HP motor that would propel the bike to speeds of 48 mph. The little two-stroke still had a hand shift, however, since CZ felt that the hand shift and hand clutch system was easier to use than those tricky little foot shift devices.

Despite its hand shifter in an era when nearly all of Europe had dropped the idea, the 125A was a smashing success. The sales charts went straight up, and CZ had to ask their 1700 workers to work overtime in an effort to keep up with the demand.

There were, of course, other manufacturers who were chasing the same market, especially in England and Germany, but the little CZ seemed to have an edge over most of these others in the marketplace. We Americans learned why in 1946 when CZ began sending their little motorcycles to our shores by the boatload. Unlike many of the others, the little "Chek" was

1939 CZ 125cc 125A

tough as nails and always an easy starter. The direct generator-to-lights lighting may have dimmed to a candle at low revs, and the rigid framed little beast may have ridden like a buckboard, but by darn the little buzzbomb never let you down. They always ran and they never broke.

The engine required a 1 to 15 mixture of oil to the gasoline, which was easily measured in the small cup on the bottom of the fuel tank cap, which was then run through the little motor with its distinctive twin exhaust pipes and fishtail mufflers.

There was no speedometer on these 125A models, and the tiny five inch brakes weren't very powerful, but we eager-eyed American kids, just like the Europeans, thought our little motorcycle was the greatest thing ever invented. They weren't very fancy, but they were willing and very tough.

When CZ entered the international markets after the war they soon found there was stiff competition for the customer's dollar. The only answer was more sophistication, which was produced in 1947 in the 125 B model with a 5 HP engine, foot shift, and huskier frame and fork. In 1948 the 125BT model had a non-hydraulically dampened telescopic front fork, which was followed by a plunger rear suspension model in 1950. A swing-arm frame was used in 1954, after

which CZ went on to become famous for their great moto-cross machines. Their road models continue and carry forth the East European ideal of simplicity, low cost, and durability.

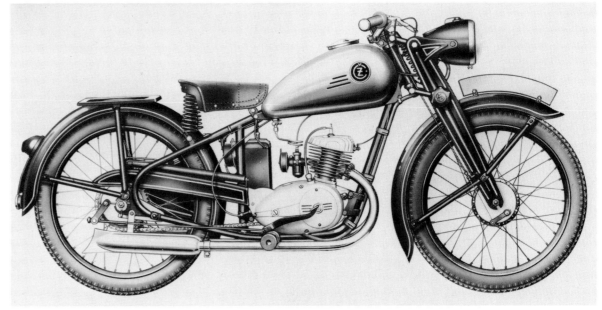

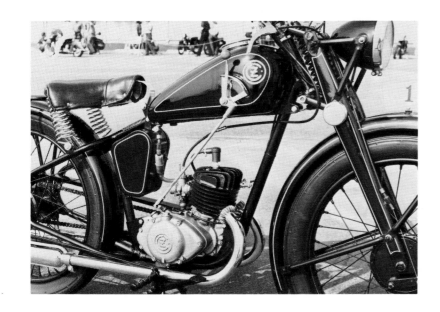

Technical Specifications

Engine:	Single cylinder, two stroke. Bore and stroke 54 x 54mm, 125cc. Cast-iron cylinder and alloy head. Roller bearing rod. Compression ratio 6.0 to 1. Jikov 18mm carburetor. Generator ignition. 4.5 HP at 4500 rpm.
Chassis:	Single loop frame, rigid. Girder front fork.
Transmission:	Primary and secondary chains. Hand shift. Ratios 7.0, 11.7, and 22.1 to 1.
Tires:	2.75 x 19 inch front and rear.
Brakes:	1.0 x 5.0 inches, drum type.
Fuel tank:	2.0 gallons.
Dimensions:	Wheelbase 48 inches. Weight 180 pounds.
Speed:	48 mph.

1946 Triumph 500cc Speed Twin
England

DURING THE LATE 1930s the European motorcycle was progressing rapidly in technical excellence. The newest machine tools allowed the factories to work to finer tolerances and produce smaller parts with precision, which combined with the general increase in engineering knowledge to produce some increasingly sophisticated designs.

England was the undisputed leader then with a wide variety of single, twin, and four-cylinder road models, plus a great array of more specialized machines for trials, scrambles, sports road use, and road racing. The now classic British single ruled supreme, with virtues of simplicity, low production cost, durability, performance, and fine handling.

The big British single had some serious limitations, however, with the hard starting and substantial vibration being the most obvious. Many attempts had been made to produce some 500cc multi-cylinder models, but all failed due to high production costs, a lack of durability, or a bulky appearance that did little to enhance the handling — a virtue that will always be the single's greatest asset.

One of those trying to produce a good twin was Triumph. An old company with roots dating back to 1885 as a bicycle manufacturer, Triumph got into the motorcycle game in 1902 with a Minerva (Belgian) powered motorbike. During the 1920s some very good singles were produced, followed by a 650cc Vertical twin 1933 that was a failure. The twin was too bulky and had a hand shift in an era when the foot shift had become accepted practice in England, which helped kill the design.

Triumph was virtually bankrupt in 1936 when Jack Sangster bought the company. One of Sangster's first moves was to hire Edward Turner to design a whole new range of motorcycles, since Turner had done so well in rescuing the Ariel concern from financial disaster when he designed the famous Square Four and the Red Hunter single.

The first of Turner's new designs made their debut in 1937 in the form of 250, 350, and 500cc singles. These OHV thumpers were produced in both standard and sports stages of tune and trim, with the sporting Tiger 70, 80, and 90 models also being offered in trials trim.

Turner's most brilliant work was yet to come, however, since it was not until 1938 that he revolutionized the motorcycle industry with his 500cc Speed Twin. A vertical twin with two pistons that rose and fell in unison, the new Triumph was a smashing success in the marketplace and assured the financial future of the company. The basic design is still in use today, and was widely copied by other manufacturers after the war.

Turner was proud of his new twin and told the world it was superior to the singles because it could be run at higher revs with less stress on the components, run smoother at low revs, was more durable, was easier to start, and cost little more to produce than the thumpers. The "more durable" claim was highly suspect, but the easier starting and smoother running

1946 Triumph 500cc Speed Twin

claims were certainly true and were a strong selling feature on the sales floor.

Perhaps the most significant thing about the new design was that it was so small and compact. By using single castings for the head and cylinder, Turner kept the crankcase very narrow. No center main bearing was used, with the two cranks being bolted to the central flywheel. The new engine was, in fact, so narrow that Turner was able to use the frame from the Tiger 90 single without even altering the rear chain line. This lack of a center main bearing worked well on the 500, but many years later the increase in engine size to 650 and 750cc with more power and revs yielded a high level of vibration that other manufacturers quieted down with a central main bearing and even auxiliary balancer shafts.

The first Speed Twin had a rigid frame and a girder front fork and weighed only 365 pounds. With a mild 7.0 to 1 compression ratio and small 15/16 inch carburetor it would run a healthy 90 mph, yet it was very flexible at low speeds. A faster Tiger 100 model was added to the range in 1939, which had a top speed of 100 mph. The Tiger 100 was a sporting motorcycle, and many owners removed the end caps from the megaphone-type mufflers to get 34 HP at 7000 rpm and a top speed of 105 mph. Ridden to work

during the week, the new Tiger 100 made a superb weekend roadracer.

The Speed Twin shown here is a 1946 model with the telescopic front fork that Triumph developed during the war for the military models. In 1947 Triumph offered their new "Spring Hub" that provided several inches of rear suspension, which made the twin a comfortable bike to ride. Stylish and a delight to ride, the Speed

Twin ushered in a whole new concept of motorcycling.

Technical Specifications

Engine:	Vertical twin, overhead valve. Bore and stroke 63 x 80mm, 500cc. Cast-iron cylinder and head. Plain bearing rods. Compression ratio 7.0 to 1. Amal 15/16 inch carburetor. Lucas magneto ignition. 26 HP at 6000 rpm.
Chassis:	Single loop, cradle frame, rigid. Telescopic front fork.
Transmission:	Primary and secondary chains. Foot shift. Ratios 5.0, 6.0, 8.65, and 12.70 to 1.
Tires:	3.25 x 19 inch front and rear.
Brakes:	1-1/8 x 7.0 inches, drum type.
Fuel tank:	4.8 gallons.
Dimensions:	Wheelbase 54 inches. Weight 365 pounds.
Speed:	90 mph.

1947 Norton 500cc International
England

ONE OF THE MOST exciting aspects of the British industry in the 1930s was the marketing of many "sports" models that possessed a superior design and performance than the standard touring models. England continued this practice after the war and produced some exotic bikes that have now become great classics.

The idea was to produce a "street replica" of a racing model for the connoisseur who didn't mind paying a premium price for a bike with technically superior specifications. Many owners used these bikes for fast road work or "play racer," while others stripped them down and used them for either Clubman racing for stock designs or in pure-sang road racing events.

Norton was one of those who produced such a machine. In those days Norton fielded a works team on 350 and 500cc OHC singles that made history with every outing. They also produced a replica racer called the International before the war and the Manx after the war. The post-war International became a sporting model with

a pedigree that traced directly to the Isle of Man and victory. Pure prestige.

The 1947 International shown here is one of those bikes. Offered in both 350 and 500cc sizes, the International featured the plunger type of rear suspension that Norton first used on their works racers in 1936. In 1938 the replica racer was produced with this frame, which was then offered on the roadsters in 1939. A popular suspension system with many manufacturers after the war, the plunger design used springs but no hydraulic damping.

Norton was also a pioneer of the telescopic front fork, which they first used in 1938 on their works racers in undampened form. Hydraulic damping was added in 1947 when all Nortons came with the "Roadholder" fork, which was surely the best fork ever produced until the Ceriani types of the 1960s.

When an enthusiast purchased an "Inter" he was not buying just snob appeal. He was acquiring an incredibly good motorcycle that was capable of running 95 to 100 mph in bog stock tune and up

to 105 mph when set up for clubman racing or true road racing events. Despite its speed, the most remarkable virtue of the Inter was the durability of the overhead cam engine. With a design heritage that stretched back to the first Norton cammers in 1927, the 1947 single contained everything Norton had learned about how to keep a high speed engine in one piece for a long distance road race.

The whole motorcycle reflected this quest of durability. The frame was built like a bridge, the engine had a massive crankcase with huge bearings, the fork tubes were immense, the fenders were stout to withstand vibration, the tanks were both rubber mounted, and the gearbox was all but indestructible — even if it did shift with a loud "clunk." The Inter was, therefore, no featherweight — weighing in at 390 pounds.

There was nothing extraordinary about the engine. It was a straightforward OHC single with massive and polished parts everywhere. The drive to the single camshaft was by a vertical shaft and two pairs

1947 Norton 500cc International

of bevel gears, with the hairpin valve-springs left exposed for cooling. In the early days the poor spring steels suffered from heat and often fractured, which gave Norton a hangup about covering up the springs from the cool blast of air. The last Manx racers, in 1963, still had their springs exposed!

The Inter had the finest goodies available then. A 1-5/32 inch Amal TT carburetor was fitted, as was a Lucas hand advance magneto. In order to provide adequate cornering clearance when heeled over, Norton fitted a 21 inch front wheel and 20 inch rear wheel. Standard seven inch brakes were used, but some owners installed a huge conical front hub from a Manx with an eight inch binder to get stopping power to match the speed.

Like their great rival, the Velocette, Norton rated their engines conservatively. The 500cc single was rated at 29 HP at 5500 rpm, but a 100 mph speed had the engine turning over at 5800 rpm on the tall 4.64 to 1 gear ratio. At this speed the single would run forever, despite the hand-numbing vibration level.

The International had some problems, however, and the most objectionable was the hard starting. It caused strong men to weep. Kicking the big single over required a terrible stomping on the kickstarter, and if the spark lever was not set just right the rider could be administered a terrible beating on the leg. Another objection was the oil that ran down from the exposed valve gear, which soon covered the bike and often the rider. Such trivialities are of little concern to those who treasure these great classics today, since they bring their owners much nostalgia and fetch incredible prices on the market. A motorcycle with a pedigree.

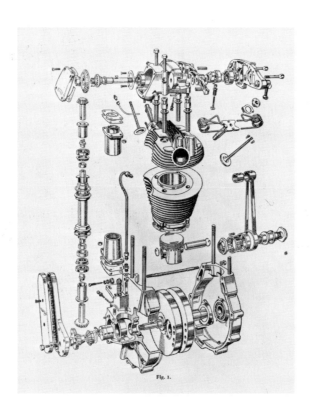

Fig. 1.

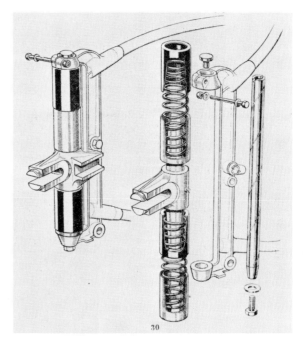

30

 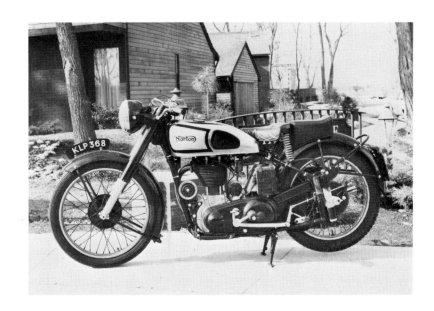

Technical Specifications

Engine:	Single cylinder, overhead camshaft. Bore and Stroke 79 x 100mm, 500cc. Cast-iron cylinder and head, alloy parts optional. Roller bearing rod. Compression ratio 7.12 to 1. Amal 1-5/32 inch TT carburetor. Lucas magneto ignition. 29 HP at 5500 rpm.
Chassis:	Single loop, cradle frame, plunger suspension. Telescopic fork.
Transmission:	Primary and secondary chains. Foot shift. Ratios 4.64, 5.1, 6.18, and 10.8 to 1.
Tires:	3.00 x 21 inch front, 3.25 x 20 inch rear.
Brakes:	1-1/4 x 7.0 inches, drum type.
Fuel tank:	4-1/2 gallons.
Dimensions:	Wheelbase 54-3/4 inches. Weight 390 pounds.
Speed:	95-100 mph.

1949 Ariel 500cc Red Hunter
England

FOR PURE BEAUTY of line, it would be hard to beat the 1949 Ariel Red Hunter. The product of an age when single cylinders ruled supreme, the Red Hunter matched an exceptional beauty with an uncommon amount of mechanical virtue.

The Red Hunter models first saw the light of day in 1933 when Ariel introduced a new line of single-cylinder bikes in both standard and sports stages of tune. The 500cc Red Hunter was the sports model, and it was soon followed by a 350cc version and then a 250 in 1935. Intended to be a fast mount for the rider who liked to thump rapidly down a winding English lane, the Red Hunters had a spirited performance without being bad mannered.

Fitted with a faster cam, larger valves, polished ports, and a larger 1-1/8 inch carburetor, the 500cc single developed 27 HP at 5500 rpm and ran 90 mph. The Red Hunters were available with either a single or two-port head and exhaust system, with many riders favoring the optional upswept exhaust pipes that allowed off-road use for weekend play.

The idea behind the Red Hunter was to provide a faster bike than the standard touring models, which made it suitable for both daily transportation and weekend use in competition events. Many owners used their Ariels for road racing on the short circuits, where a megaphone exhaust and the optional 7.5 to 1 compression ratio (6.5 was standard) would yield a 100 mph speed. The brakes were also larger than normal to handle the speed, with the drums having cast-on fins to dissipate the heat.

In 1935 the company offered a competition model — a practice coming into popularity in England then. The "comp" model was a road model fitted with a 21 inch front wheel, knobby tires, a big 4.00 inch rear tire, a crankcase shield, a smaller 2.5 gallon fuel tank, upswept exhaust, and lower gearing. The Red Hunter comp model was a superb trials bike and won dozens of major events, including the 1938 Scottish Six Days Trial.

The original design was improved in 1936 when a cannister was fitted to the valve gear to cover it up, followed by a new head in 1937 which had alloy boxes over the valve gear to make the engine fully oil tight. In 1938 came a quickly detachable rear wheel, followed in 1939 by a new plunger rear suspension that worked on swivel links in an effort to move the axle in an arc and thus maintain constant chain tension. Each Red Hunter had polished flywheels and connecting rod, and each engine was bench tested before it left the works.

The pre-war Red Hunters established a superb record in English trials and scrambles events, and they also gave their owners a chance to go road racing on weekends — even if they were a little slower than the pukka OHC AJS, Excelsior, Norton, and Velocette racers. Perhaps the most amazing feat occurred in Australia where Art Senior set a new Aussie speed record of 127.63 mph with his alcohol burning Red Hunter — a speed that even the factory found hard to believe.

After the war, Ariel resumed production

1949 Ariel 500cc Red Hunter

in 1946, but the 250cc Red Hunter was dropped. In 1947 a telescopic front fork replaced the old girder fork, and then in 1950 came Ariel's first pure sang competition model. Stripped for action, the new rigid frame 500cc VCH or Competition Red Hunter had an alloy engine with special cams to provide 25 HP at 6000 rpm on a 6.8 to 1 compression ratio. Weighing only 290 pounds and with a steep steering geometry for fine balance and handling in trials events, the comp model had wide ratio gears of 6.05, 9.16, 12.6, and 19.1 to 1. Close ratio gears were also available for scrambles use, but the new VCH was really intended for trials events.

In 1952 came the VHA road model with alloy engine, but in 1953 this idea was dropped in favor of a cast-iron cylinder and alloy head on all models except the VCH, which retained the alloy cylinder. In 1954 the plunger frame was dropped in favor of a swinging-arm design, and then in 1956 a set of full-width alloy hubs were used. A fire breathing 500cc scrambler made its debut in 1954, followed by a new spring frame 500cc HT trials model in 1956. The works trials team had used prototype springers in 1955, and these two competition models helped usher in the era of highly specialized British motorcycles for every type of competition. Weighing only 290

pounds, the HT became famous in the hands of Sammy Miller, who got his bike down to only 242 pounds by using many fiberglass and alloy parts.

The 1949 Red Hunter shown here is thus a motorcycle with a heritage of sports road use, road racing by "clubmen" riders, moto-cross, and historic wins in trials events. As a roadster it offered a superior performance without being radical, and its elegant lines and exceptional aesthetics have given it an enviable place in the story of the motorcycle. Produced near the end of the rigid frame era, the 1949 Red Hunter is everything that British motorcycles used to be.

THE RED HUNTER
350 c.c. MODEL NH £57-10

Equipped with Lucas Lighting and Electric Horn.

Technical Specifications

Engine:	Single cylinder, overhead valve. Bore and stroke 81.8 x 95mm, 500cc. Cast-iron cylinder and head. Roller bearing rod. Compression ratio 6.8 to 1. Amal 1-1/8 inch carburetor. Lucas magneto. 24.6 HP at 6000 rpm.
Chassis:	Single loop frame, rigid. Telescopic front fork.
Transmission:	Primary and secondary chains. Foot shift. Ratios 4.7, 6.0, 8.0, and 12.5 to 1.
Tires:	3.00 x 20 inch front, 3.25 x 19 inch rear.
Brakes:	1-1/4 x 7.0 inches, drum type.
Fuel tank:	3-3/4 gallons.
Dimensions:	Wheelbase 56 inches. Weight 375 pounds.
Speed:	90 mph.

1949 Indian 220cc Arrow
America

WHEN WORLD WAR II ended the Indian Motorcycle Company was in a poor state of financial health. They had not done well on their military contracts due to poor management, and then they were faced with the new threat of foreign competition for the first time in the history of their company.

In 1945 Ralph B. Rogers, a self-made millionaire industrialist, took over as president and began implementing many of his progressive ideas into the stagnant company. Production of civilian models resumed in the spring of 1946, with the big Chief being the only model produced. The Chief was updated with a new hydraulically dampened girder front fork that greatly enhanced the handling over the earlier leaf-spring fork model, yet Rogers correctly reasoned that Indian could never survive very long on this old design.

What Rogers had his eye on was the rising horde of motorcycles being imported from Europe. In 1946, for instance, Indian sold 2800 Chiefs, but the Europeans sold 9064 bikes in America. A total of 8596 of these came from England, and therein lies the tale. The light, nimble handling, and foot-shifted British bikes were so much more fun to ride than the huge American machines, and they also performed much better in the many forms of off-road play that were becoming popular then.

Rogers had great vision and realized that the days of the huge side-valve V-twin were numbered. The small foreign bikes were appealing to so many more people than the monstrous American machines — a trend that was accelerated in 1948 when England devalued their pound sterling from $4.05 to $2.80 and was thus able to offer British bikes at prices well below those of the Harley and Indian.

Rogers began working on his plan to produce a lightweight Indian when his company purchased the Torque Engineering Company in July of 1945. The Torque company had designed some new lightweights along British lines, and Rogers thought this was the way to go. The prototypes included an eleven inch single and a 22 inch vertical twin, but these were soon punched out to 13 and 26 cubic inches.

In October of 1946 the new lightweight Indians were announced, and the first bikes soon rolled off the assembly lines. The little 220cc single featured a rigid frame, but the 440cc twin had a plunger rear suspension. Weighing only 220 and 285 pounds and with a telescopic front fork and foot shift-hand clutch design, the new Indians were both attractive and appealing.

The new OHV Indians were a disaster, however, with magneto failures and rod bearing failures being the most common. The resultant publicity was so bad that Indian halted production in 1947 to redesign the bikes, after which production resumed in 1948.

Called the 220cc Arrow and 440cc Scout, the 1948 models were a little stronger than the first machines but still not anywhere as durable as the traditional Indian V-twin or the British bikes. The

1949 Indian 220cc Arrow

basic design looked good on paper with two cams, external pushrod tubes, alloy cylinders and heads, and plain-bearing rods on a built-up crankshaft. Quite similar to the Triumph Speed Twin in design, the Scout used an Amal carburetor and British looking controls.

In 1949 the Arrow was offered in both rigid frame and spring frame versions, and

then in 1950 the twin was punched out to 500cc and the little single was phased out. The twin staggered on until 1952 when it, too, was dropped from production just one year before Indian halted production of the grand old Chief.

The pretty little Arrow shown here is a 1949 model with the spring frame. Fitted with 3.25 x 18 inch tires and available in red, black, yellow, green, or blue paint schemes, the little thumper was a most attractive bike. The performance was re-

spectable, too, with a 60 to 65 mph top speed and brisk acceleration through the four-speed gearbox.

The durability was still a problem, though, which was surely due to the extremely light construction of the whole motorcycle. The concept of a lightweight

Indian was good, but the execution left much to be desired. The designers went too far in reducing the weight and ended up with a fragile machine. Attractive and visionary, the Indian lightweights passed into history as the most embarrassing chapter in the history of the company.

Technical Specifications

Engine:	Single cylinder, overhead valve. Bore and stroke 2-3/8 x 3.0 inches, 216.5cc. Alloy cylinder and head. Plain bearing rod. Compression ratio 7.0 to 1. Linkert carburetor. Edison magneto. Estimated 10 HP at 5500 rpm.
Chassis:	Single loop, cradle frame, plunger suspension. Telescopic fork.
Transmission:	Primary and secondary chains. Foot shift. Ratios 6.12, 7.4, 11.69, and 17.0 to 1.
Tires:	3.25 x 18 inch front and rear.
Brakes:	1.0 x 6-1/2 inches, drum type.
Fuel tank:	4.0 gallons.
Dimensions:	Wheelbase 52 inches. Weight 220 pounds.
Speed:	60-65 mph.

1952 Vincent 1000cc Rapide
England

ONE OF THE MOST remarkable motorcycles ever produced was the Vincent. Manufactured in England from 1928 to late 1955, the Vincent is now one of the world's most sought-after classics.

Intended to be a high performance motorcycle of exceptional quality, the Vincent is best remembered for its speed. The 1000cc Rapide, for instance, was rated at 110-115 mph, while the fabulous Black Shadow would run 125. The alcohol burning Black Lightning was claimed to run 150 mph, which was proven in America when Rollie Free broke the American speed record of 136.183 mph when he clocked 150.313 mph at Bonneville in 1948 and 156.58 in 1950. The previous record had been set by a 1000cc Harley-Davidson in 1937.

In the post-war years the Vincent Company advertised that "the Vincent is the fastest standard motorcycle in the world." Nobody ever argued with that claim. One American magazine tested a Black Shadow in 1952 and clocked a speed of 128.57 mph with a box-stock bike. It was

many years later in the 1970s before any stock motorcycle was to better this speed.

The brainchild of enthusiast-designer Philip Vincent, the Vincent-HRD came to life out of the old HRD. Produced by Howard R. Davies, who won the 1925 Senior TT on one of his bikes, the HRD was a reasonably good motorbike that used the J.A.P. engines. Vincent bought the HRD in 1928, after which he continued the use of J.A.P. engines until he began production of his own 500cc engine in 1934. The single was followed in 1936 by the first 1000cc V-twin Rapide, which was really the beginning of the Vincent legend. Vincent kept the HRD name on his bikes until 1949, at which time it became just "The Vincent."

The real reason why Vincent purchased the HRD Company was not speed, however, but rather to give him a going company and machine upon which to apply his pet theory — a spring frame. Convinced that the motorcycle would never gain wide public acceptance until it was more comfortable to ride, Vincent offered

his first springers in 1928 when spring frames were virtually unheard of.

The Vincent design had the whole rear frame section moving against a large coil spring beneath the seat. The triangulated frame section had about three to four inches of travel, but the lack of hydraulic damping made for a rather bouncy action.

The first 1000cc twin ran on a 6.8 to 1 compression ratio and pumped out 45 HP at 5500 rmp. With a pair of 1-1/16 inch carburetors and a long 90mm stroke, the engine had lots of torque, which enabled it to pull a very tall 3.8 to 1 top gear ratio and run 110 mph. The big twin bristled with Vincent's innovative ideas, including dual brakes on each wheel that provided stopping power to match the speed.

This first Vincent Rapide had a Burman gearbox and Brampton girder front fork, but the Burman box was dropped in 1946 when the new Series B replaced the pre-war Series A models. Totally redesigned to clean up the Series A engine with its many external oil lines and fittings, the Series B had the engine and gearbox in

1952 Vincent 1000cc Rapide

one large case. Vincent even designed his own clutch, which had centrifugally operated shoes to assist the friction process. This clutch was destined to become the Achilles heel of the Vincent.

In 1948 the Series C was introduced that had the new Girdraulic front fork. Designed to retain the precise steering qualities of the girder fork with its great torsional stiffness, the new fork had a spring-oil shock absorber that provided the advantage of hydraulic damping. The Girdraulic fork was extremely stable at speed and proved to be the perfect mate for the speedy powerplant.

The Vincent shown here is a 1952 Series C Rapide, which was a more suitable bike for city streets and touring than the more highly tuned Black Shadow. With a 7.3 to 1 compression ratio and larger 1-1/8 inch carburetors, the Black Shadow developed 55 HP at 5700 rpm and pulled a 3.5 to 1 top gear ratio. With alloy cylinders and heads painted black, the big Vincent weighed only 458 pounds.

In 1954 the Series D was introduced, which included two radically styled Black Prince and Black Knight models which had the rear two-thirds of the motorcycle enclosed in a fiberglass body. The Series D also had coil ignition and only one brake on the rear wheel. By then the Vincent had become so expensive that sales

had fallen to where the business was no longer profitable, so the great legacy of speed became just a legend.

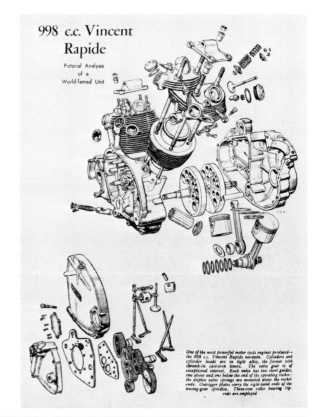

998 c.c. Vincent Rapide

Pictorial Analysis of a World-famed Unit

One of the most powerful motor cycle engines produced—the 998 c.c. Vincent Rapide vee-twin. Cylinders and cylinder heads are in light alloy, the former with shrunk-in cast-iron liners. The valve gear is of exceptional interest. Each valve has two short guides, one above and one below the end of the operating rocker; the duplex valve springs are mounted about the rocker ends. Outrigger plates carry the right-hand ends of the timing-gear spindles. Three-row roller bearing big-ends are employed.

Technical Specifications

Engine:	V-twin, overhead valve. Bore and stroke 84 x 90mm, 1000cc. Alloy cylinders and heads. Roller bearing rods. Compression ratio 6.45 to 1. Two Amal 1-1/16 inch carburetors. Lucas magneto ignition. 45 HP at 5300 rpm.
Chassis:	Tubular space frame, pivoted fork suspension. Girdraulic fork.
Transmission:	Primary and secondary chains. Foot shift. Ratios 3.5, 4.16, 5.64, and 9.1 to 1.
Tires:	3.00 x 20 inch front, 3.50 x 19 inch rear.
Brakes:	1.0 x 7.0 inches, dual drum type.
Fuel tank:	4.0 gallons.
Dimensions:	Wheelbase 56-1/2 inches. Weight 455 pounds.
Speed:	110-115 mph.

1955 BSA 500cc Gold Star
England

DURING THE MIDDLE 1950s a subtle change came over the European motorcycle scene. The Germans and Italians began dominating the grand prix scene with exotic multi-cylinder racers, and their technically advanced 50 to 250cc lightweights also began to sell by the millions.

England dropped out of the grand prix game then to adopt a philosophy of producing specialized motorcycles for a wide variety of sporting uses and let the continentals build the exotic works GP bikes. England's dominance of the world championships thus came to an end, but the common man benefited mightily due to the great variety of specialized production models he could buy.

One such model was the 1955 BSA Gold Star. Intended to be suitable for either the clubman races for standard sports road models or as an ultra-sporting roadster, the Gold Star was nothing less than a road racer with lights. First produced in 1938 in 500cc form as the model M24, the Gold Star was not produced after the war until a 350cc model

was introduced in 1949. The 71 x 88mm 350cc single was pushed out to an 85mm bore in 1950 for 500cc, with the Goldie being offered in road, trials, scrambles, clubman racing, or pure road racing versions.

In 1953 the original plunger frame model was dropped in favor of a new swinging-arm version, which was followed in 1954 by the CB series with massively finned cylinder and head. In less than one year the DB series was introduced with a huge 1-1/2 inch Amal GP carburetor, followed in 1956 by the DBD series with many small technical improvements. A special 2.0 inch by 190mm front brake was offered for racing as early as 1955, which was later adopted on the Clubman model. Housed in a full-width alloy hub, this brake had an extractor fan for cooling the hub.

The BSA Gold Star was very successful in the Isle of Man Clubman TT races for standard street-legal motorcycles. They first won the Junior Clubman TT in 1949, and then went on to win every race until

the last in 1956. In the Senior Clubman TT they first won in 1954 at 85.76 mph; a record speed. The new DBD model was running 115 mph by then with 42 HP at 7000 rpm, with the road racer being clocked up to 125 mph. Both the 350 and 500cc singles gained many places in the top six in major road races — an incredible performance for a pushrod design!

The Gold Stars did well in the dirt, too, winning the 1951 and 1955 Scottish Six Days Trials, the 1955 world moto-cross championship, and dozens of major American track and cross-country events. The trials Goldies were rigid frame models until the works bikes of 1955, after which BSA produced a spring frame trials bike in 1956.

The American dirt track riders loved the Gold Star, and great efforts were made by many tuners to extract the last ounce of power from the engines. Several succeeded in getting as much as 50 HP at engine speeds up to 8000 rpm, but then the typical American race was of a much

1955 BSA 500cc Gold Star

shorter distance than the European road races where reliability was so important.

The Clubman Gold Star sent to America was a different breed than the British version. In England the Goldie was set up for clubman racing or very fast road work with taller close-ratio gears, rearset footpegs, and clip-on handlebars, while the American "touring" version had standard pegs and bars, a smaller 2-1/2 gallon fuel tank, and gear ratios of 5.0, 6.05, 8.79, and 12.9 to 1. A 5.0 gallon knee-knotched alloy fuel tank was available for road racing, as was a wide selection of cams and compression ratios.

During its life the Gold Star had some problems, the most serious being the common connecting-rod breakage that always destroyed the crankcase. The drive-side mainshaft also loved to pull out of the flywheel, and then the vibration was so bad that the carburetor float had to be remotely mounted on rubber bushings to prevent the fuel from frothing.

The starting procedure was also something to try a man's patience. With the huge carburetor, a high compression ratio, and a racing cam, the Goldie was difficult to start and disinclined to run at all below 2000 rpm. In a sense it was really too radical for street use, since big singles acquire some very unpleasant habits when made too radical.

The handling was also not the best, due partly to the heavy 410 pound weight and the top-heavy handling at "town" speeds with the clip-on bars. The Gold Star went like blazes, though, and to this day there is a devoted clan of riders who insist it was the last real motorcycle England produced. Never a bike for the faint-of-heart, the Gold Star continued to win dirt track races in America long after the factory ceased production in 1963. A temperamental beast, the Gold Star fell victim to the trend of larger twin-cylinder motorcycles that went just as fast but with little fuss.

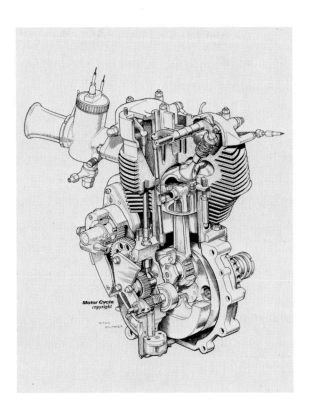

B.S.A. 500 c.c. O.H.V. Gold Star
Model M 24

The now famous B.S.A. Gold Star — the fastest standard sports machine you can buy. It is fitted with **quickly detachable rear wheel**.

£77. 10s.
Competition model £5 extra.

Speedometer extra.

All machines supplied with speedometer unless otherwise ordered.

Technical Specifications

Engine:	Single cylinder, overhead valve. Bore and stroke 85 x 88mm, 500cc. Alloy cylinder and head. Roller bearing rod. Compression ratio 8.8 to 1. Amal 1-1/2 inch GP carburetor. Lucas magneto. 42 HP at 7000 rpm.
Chassis:	Twin loop, cradle frame, swinging arm suspension. Telescopic fork.
Transmission:	Primary and secondary chains. Foot shift. Ratios: Clubman- 4.52, 4.96, 5.99, and 8.71 to 1. Touring- 5.0, 6.05, 8.79, and 12.9 to 1.
Tires:	3.00 x 19 or 3.00 x 21 inch front, 3.50 x 19 inch rear.
Brakes:	1.0 x 8.0 inches front, 1.0 x 7.0 inches rear. Drum type.
Fuel tank:	4-1/2 gallons.
Dimensions:	Wheelbase 56 inches. Weight 410 pounds.
Speed:	115 mph.

1957 Matchless 350cc G3LC
England

ONE OF THE MOST interesting aspects of the years just after World War II was the emergence of trials and moto-cross as major international sports. Prior to the war the British had produced some competition versions of their road models, which were used in both trials and scrambles events. The scrambles game spread to the continent in the late 1930s, and then after the war the two-heat moto-cross system came into use and quickly grew into a European Championship in 1952 and then on into a full World Championship in 1957.

The trials sport had its birth in the very early days and was a reliability contest to test the durability of the machines rather than the skill of the riders. By the 1930s it had evolved into a true sport, however, in which the riders rode to the trials, removed the lights, and then competed over a tough creek-bottom course, after which they installed their lights for the ride home.

The British loved their trials and produced even more specialized trials bikes after the war with wide-ratio gears, upswept exhaust pipes, knobby tires, and alloy fenders. Lights were fitted at first, but by 1950 most companies had dropped the electrics to produce a nimble handling bike in pure competition form. Special cams were used to give lots of low speed power, which combined with long-stroke engines and heavy flywheels to provide the ultimate in "plonking" ability over the rocks. Alloy cylinders and heads came into use, with special frames to provide a steep fork angle for ultra-slow speed balance.

Weighing a little under 300 pounds, these machines helped the sport to grow in stature until it spread to the continent in the late 1950s. In 1964 the Henri Grouters Challenge Cup series was introduced, which was tantamount to a European Championship. The sport continued to grow, with the F.I.M. elevating it to a formal European Championship in 1968. The British riders did not take too much interest in this series until 1975 when the F.I.M. made it a World Championship,

since the sport had been so "English" up to then that there was more prestige in winning the British Championship than in winning the European title.

During these years there was one trials event which was to the trials game as the Isle of Man was to road racing — the Scottish Six Days Trial. Held in the highlands over nearly 500 miles of roads and rock-strewn trails, the Scottish is still the premier event in the world.

The rugged terrain in the Scottish placed a great emphasis on durable machinery. The rocks loved to bash bikes to pieces, which suited the AJS and Matchless riders just fine. An old company dating back to before 1900, Matchless bought the AJS company in 1931 and then amalgamated the two lines with their new "G" series of singles in 1936. From then until the final days of their singles in the middle 1960s, the only difference between AJS and Matchless was the name tag and the timing covers on the engine.

In 1946 the two marques were again in production, with competition models soon

1957 Matchless 350cc G3LC

available for trials use. In 1950 came new alloy-engined bog wheels in 350 and 500cc sizes, which had rigid frames and a 296 pound weight. It took a long time for spring frames to be accepted in the trials game, but in 1955 Associated Motor Cycles Ltd. decided to follow the Royal Enfield lead and mount their works team on springers. The spring frame models worked to perfection, which prompted the factory to produce the 350cc Matchless G3LC and AJS 16C with the new frame in 1956.

These were superb trials bikes with incredible low speed plonking power, which were then steadily improved until the last bikes were produced in 1965. In 1957 AMC produced their own gearbox to replace the earlier Burman box, and then in 1958 a new frame was used that provided ten inches of ground clearance. Tiny five inch brakes were adopted in 1959, which helped reduce the weight from 320 to 306 pounds.

During these years AJS and Matchless dominated the Scottish with ten wins in the 19 years from 1947 to 1965. Hugh Viney scored his epic ''hat trick'' in 1947-48-49 on an AJS, followed by Artie Ratcliffe's win in 1950 on a Matchless. Viney won again in 1953, as did Ratcliffe in 1954. Gordon Jackson then rode his AJS to wins in 1956, 1958, 1960, and

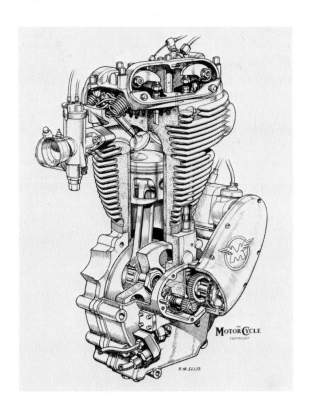

1961. In 1961 his works bike weighed only 245 pounds and had plonking power of a type that enabled him to trickle over the boulders at a snail's pace. Gordon scored his historic ''one point'' ride that year in edging out the great Sammy Miller on his 500cc Ariel. All of these wins were on 350s, and the 1961 win by Jackson is still the greatest ride the Scottish has ever known.

The days of the classic big single were numbered, however, with the first blow struck in 1959 when Roy Peplow won the Scottish on a tiny 200cc Triumph. Sammy Miller switched to a 250cc Bultaco in 1965 to score the first ever win by a two-stroke, after which the big 350 and 500cc thumpers quickly faded from the highlands. The classic era was ended.

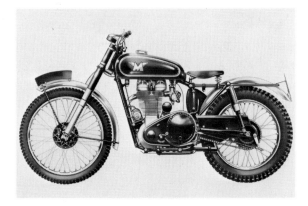

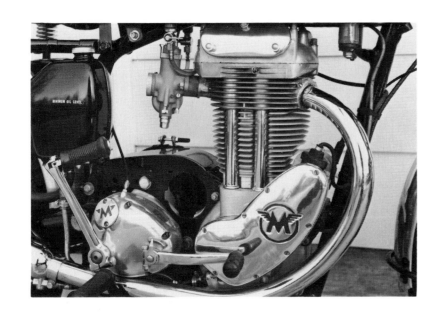 

Technical Specifications

Engine:	Single cylinder, overhead valve. Bore and stroke 69 x 93mm, 350cc. Alloy cylinder and head. Roller bearing rod. Compression ratio 6.5 to 1. Amal 1-1/16 inch carburetor. Lucas competition magneto. 18 HP at 5750 rpm.
Chassis:	Single loop, cradle frame, swinging arm suspension. Telescopic fork.
Transmission:	Primary and secondary chains. Foot shift. Ratios 6.5, 9.6, 15.5, and 21.3 to 1.
Tires:	2.75 x 21 inch front, 4.00 x 19 inch rear.
Brakes:	1.0 x 7.0 inches, drum type.
Fuel tank:	2.0 gallons.
Dimensions:	Wheelbase 54 inches. Weight 320 pounds.
Speed:	65 mph.

1959 Parilla 250cc Super Sport
Italy

FOR PURE ART on wheels, no one can equal the Italians. Possessed with a passion for road racing, the Italians have been producing beautiful and exotic motorcycles since their industry began in earnest in the early 1920s. With a flair for superb casting and machine work, the Italians have spiced the pages of history with many beautiful road racers that are now magnificent classics.

Despite winning many grand prix races in the 1930s, the Italian manufacturers did not really come of age until the 1950s when they began to dominate the world championships. They also began selling their fast lightweights by the millions then, with many companies offering a variety of models.

One tiny company was the Parilla in Milano. Founded in 1946 by Giovanni Parilla, this company first produced a 250cc OHC single in both sports and racing versions. In 1954 a new semi-overhead cam 175cc single was produced, which was offered in *Turismo* and *Competitione* versions — the *Com-*

petitione being a little road racer with lights. A few of these Parillas came to America, which were followed in 1958 by some 200cc models and then by a 250 in 1961. A 26 HP scrambler was also produced, which had a wicked performance in the dirt.

Road racing was just getting a good start in America then, so Giovanni decided to send over his works rider with a specially prepared 250cc Super Sport to compete in the 1959 Daytona Grand Prix plus other major races. Giuseppi Rottigni was the rider, and he proceeded to win the Daytona event and show we Americans what the European riding style was all about. This brought Parilla a great deal of fame and helped sell a modest number of bikes.

One American who learned not to put his feet down in a corner as on a dirt track was Tony Woodman. Woodman took over the works Parilla and scored many wins — the last one being the 1963 Nelson Ledges National Championship. In California the team of English transplant

Ron Grant and Norris Rancourt had fast Parillas that demolished the opposition in West Coast races. In the 1964 U.S. Grand Prix at Daytona, which was an F.I.M. world championship event, Grant finished second to Alan Shepherd's MZ two-stroke from East Germany — a remarkable achievement for the little single.

The beautiful Parilla shown here is the actual Dayton winner that was ridden by Rottigni. Rarely seen in most European countries, the Parilla had a unique design which placed the camshaft very high in the tall timing case. Short pushrods were used to actuate the valves, which kept the valve gear almost as light as in an overhead cam engine. The production Super Sport racer had a chain drive to the camshaft, but this works racer had a set of finely machined gears that were mounted on needle roller bearings.

Now restored to show winning condition, the Parilla is an excellent example of 1950s Italian engineering. The engine had unit construction of the crankcase and gearbox, with a roller bearing rod working

1959 Parilla 250cc Super Sport

on a 68 x 68mm bore and stroke. Despite its fairly long stroke, the Parilla loved to rev and would scream to 10,000 rpm to pump out its 33-34 HP. This gave the bike a 115 mph top speed in unstreamlined form, and over 120 with a fairing.

The long megaphone also contributed to the mystique of the bike. The sound starts out as a deep bellow that turns into a scream as the revs mount. Loud but tolerable, the exhaust note is sheer music compared to the raspy two-strokes of today.

The sculptured fuel tank also contributes to the aesthetic effect. With knotches for the knees, the tank is a work of art. Other typically Italian design features are the helical gear primary drive, the rearset gearshift linkage, and the beautiful full-width alloy hubs. The hard starting was also typical of highly tuned Italian motorcycles from the 1950s and 1960s, which was known to cause strong men to turn to drink.

Perhaps the most striking thing about the Parilla is the color scheme. The racer is a stunning bike, and it is this that one seems to remember after having viewed the Super Sport.

Beauty does not ensure success in the marketplace, however, so that Giovanni was forced to close his doors in 1967. Beautiful and fast, the Parillas had all ac-

quired a reputation for being temperamental in an age when motorcycles were becoming sophisticated and reliable. The Yamaha two-stroke, twin-cylinder road racers were also acquiring the reliability to go with their speed, which soon made the Parilla racers obsolete. Hand built by craftsmen who were proud of their work, the Parilla Super Sport was the product of an age that has now slipped into the past.

Technical Specifications

Engine:	Single cylinder, semi overhead camshaft. Bore and stroke 68 x 68mm, 250cc. Cast iron cylinder, alloy head. Roller bearing rod. Compression ratio 10.0 to 1. Del Orto 30mm Carburetor. Magneto ignition. 33-34 HP at 10,000 rpm.
Chassis:	Single loop, cradle frame, swinging arm suspension. Telescopic fork.
Transmission:	Helical primary gears, secondary chain. Foot shift. Ratios 6.42, 7.84, 10.50, and 15.18 to 1.
Tires:	2.50 x 18 inch front, 3.00 x 18 inch rear.
Brakes:	1-1/4 x 8 inches, drum type.
Fuel tank:	3.0 gallons.
Dimensions:	Wheelbase 52 inches. Weight 235 pounds.
Speed:	115 mph.

1961 AJS 350cc 7R

England

ONE OF THE PIONEERS of the British motorcycle industry was the AJS. Founded by A. J. Stevens in 1897 to produce a four-stroke motor, the company first produced a complete motorcycle in 1909. During the 1920s the company won many TT and grand prix races, with a new overhead camshaft single making its debut in 1927.

During the 1930s the AJS race shop fielded some good singles plus a supercharged and water-cooled V-4, but it was not until 1948 that the company became a real leader when they introduced their new 350cc 7R model. Intended to be a simple OHC single which could be easily worked on by the private owners, the 7R soon acquired the affectionate name of "the boy's racer."

The 1948 7R had an ancestry dating back to the earlier R7 model of the middle 1930s and featured a simple chain drive to the single cam. Less expensive to produce than the bevel gear-and-vertical shaft drives used on the Excelsior, Norton, and Velocette, the engine developed 30 HP at 7000 rpm and ran 106 mph.

The 7R performed well and became instantly popular with the privateers — finishing 18 of 25 starters in the 1948 Junior TT. The engine was under constant development and was pushed up to 32 HP at 7200 rpm in 1949. In 1951 the compression ratio was increased from the original 8.45 to 1 to a 9.4 ratio, which boosted the output to 34 HP at 7200 revs. A change was also made from a 21 inch front and 20 inch rear tire sizes to 19 inch and rear, and clip-on bars were also used for the first time.

In 1953 the engine was made stronger with many small improvements, but the big change was a new frame with a knee-notched 5-1/2 gallon fuel tank plus a new seat with a backrest. In 1954 the works team rode 3-cam models with three valves, with New Zealander Rod Coleman winning the Junior TT on one of these "triple knocker" singles. By then the 7R was developing 37 HP at 7500 rpm.

Jack Williams then took over as de-velopment chief and set about developing the 7R even more. At the end of 1954 the company dropped their works team to concentrate on the production racer — saying that grand prix racing had become too expensive and too far removed from production practice to be of any benefit.

By conducting experiments on gas flow in various port and combustion chamber shapes and sizes, Williams was able to increase the compression ratio to 11.6 to 1. In 1956 the original 74 x 81mm bore and stroke was changed to 75.5 x 78mm, and then the carburetor size was gradually increased from 1-5/32 inch to 1-3/8 inch. The shorter stroke allowed more room for larger valves plus greater revving ability, which increased the output even more.

By 1960 the 7R was producing 42 HP at 7800 rpm and running about 120 mph in unstreamlined form and 125 with a fairing. As always, the engine was exceptionally reliable and finishing percentages of 70 to 85% were common in long distance road races. By then the weight was down

1961 AJS 350cc 7R

to only 285 pounds, and the handling had become a legend.

The speed over a twisty road racing course was impressive, with the modest single sometimes giving the world champion MV Agusta a bad time. In 1961, for instance, Mike Hailwood led the Junior TT until just 15 miles from victory when a wrist pin broke. Hailwood had been lapping in the 96-97 mph range all afternoon — a remarkable performance for an over-the-counter single-cylinder 350.

In 1954 the AMC factory (AJS and Matchless) decided to drop the Matchless G45 500cc twin and produce the 500cc G50 single. Using the same design of the 7R but with a 90 x 78mm bore and stroke, the new Matchless racer used a huge 1-1/2 inch Amal GP carburetor to produce 47 HP at 7200 rpm and run 125-127 mph in unstreamlined form. And like the 7R, the G50 became very popular with the privateers who liked the simple design that was so easy to work on in their travels all over Europe during the racing season.

All was not well at home, however, where a declining sales volume was putting pressure on the budget for the race shop. The venerable AMC roadster singles had by then outlived their popularity in a market now dominated by continental lightweights and big British twins,

and the AMC twins were not a very good design. Those were the years when economic and political forces within England were strangling their motorcycle industry, which lacked the capital to develop new designs and then tool up to produce them. The last 7Rs left the race shop in early 1963, at which time the era of British single cylinder racing motorcycles came to an end.

Technical Specifications

Engine:	Single cylinder, overhead camshaft. Bore and stroke 75.5 x 78mm, 350cc. Alloy cylinder and head. Roller bearing rod. Compression ratio 11.6 to 1. Amal 1-3/8 inch GP carburetor. Lucas racing magneto. 42 HP at 7800 rpm.
Chassis:	Twin loop, cradle frame, swinging arm suspension. Telescopic fork.
Transmission:	Primary and secondary chains. Foot shift. Ratios 4.87, 5.36, 6.46, and 8.68 to 1.
Tires:	2.75 x 19 inch front, 3.25 x 19 inch rear.
Brakes:	2.0 x 8.0 inches, drum type.
Fuel tank:	5-1/2 gallons.
Dimensions:	Wheelbase 55 inches. Weight 285 pounds.
Speed:	120 mph.

1962 Honda 305cc Super Hawk

Japan

DURING THE EARLY 1960s a change came over the world motorcycle scene of a magnitude never before experienced. It was subtle at first, but within a few years it became an avalanche that buried everything in its path.

The new force was the Japanese motorcycle industry, which before World War II barely existed. After the war there were some feeble attempts to produce some decent motorcycles, but all of these failed until the late 1950s when Soichiro Honda came along to revolutionize the industry and sport. A natural mechanical genius, Soichiro was to have a greater impact on the world motorcycle market than anyone in the history of the sport.

Born in 1906, Soichiro began producing motorbikes in 1948 with some dilapidated machine tools in a 12 x 18 wood-framed shack. In the completely disrupted Japanese society of the immediate post-war years, one of the most pressing needs was for an inexpensive mode of transportation. Honda's answer was a little 50cc clip-on motor for a bicycle. The new clip-on sold like hotcakes in transportation-starved Japan, and Honda was on his way.

In 1949 a 100cc two-stroke motorcycle was produced, which had a pressed-steel frame and looked like a 1930 German machine. Called the "D" or Dream model, this 2.3 HP single had a two-speed gearbox and was primitive by European standards. Next came the four-stroke "E" model — still primitive but selling 32,000 bikes in 1953. The 50cc Cub motorized bicycle was also produced then, followed by the 90cc Benley single. Fitted with a torsion-arm rear suspension, telescopic fork, and a 3-speed gearbox, the 3.8 HP Benley was beginning to look reasonably modern.

By then Honda realized that his machine tools were obsolete, so he borrowed over one million dollars to purchase American, German, and Swiss machinery to equip his factory. Now fully modern, Honda traveled to the Isle of Man to study European technology. Two weeks later he returned home — half in shock at just how superior European technology was to what he possessed. Undaunted, Soichiro went to work to improve his wares.

In 1955 a swinging-arm 250cc single made its debut, which was a half-decent motorcycle. The real start came in 1958, though, when Honda introduced their 50cc Super Cub — the now famous step-through model that sold by the millions. The 125cc Benley twin and 250cc Dream also made their debut then, and with these models Honda established their first distributorships in Europe and America in 1959.

These models would never have made Honda or Japan a world leader, however, since the 125 Benley was too small and the 80 mph Dream just too heavy and clumsy looking. The Dream had huge fenders, a massive pressed-steel frame, and a leading-link front fork. A modest number were sold in America along with a great number of Super Cubs, but the lack of a sporty looking motorcycle kept

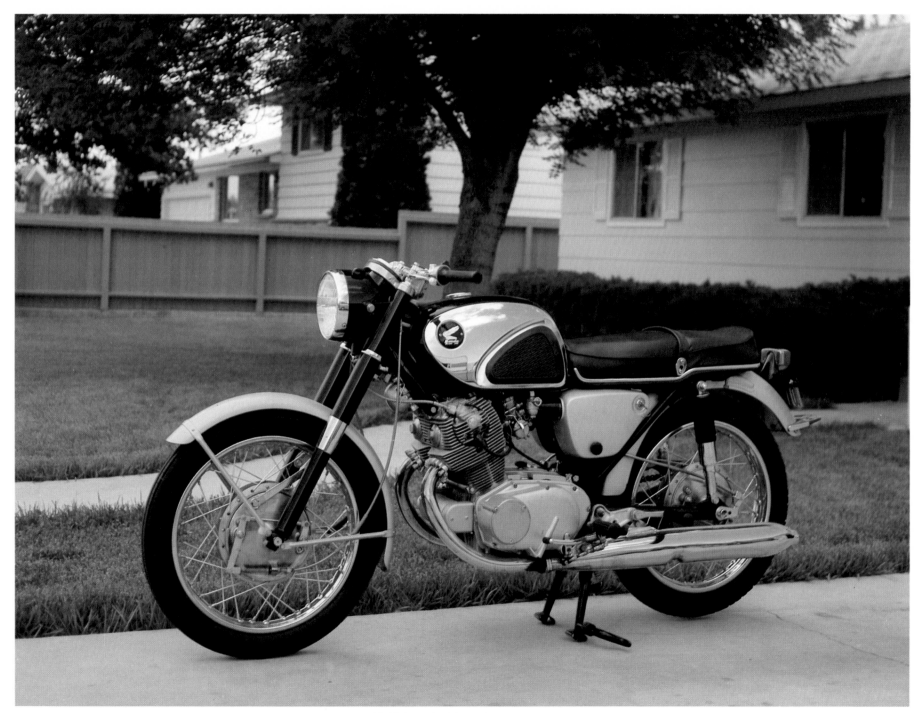

1962 Honda 305cc Super Hawk

Honda from achieving any real success in either the American or European markets.

Honda rectified this situation in 1962 with a sports version of the 250cc Dream called the Hawk, plus a new 305cc Super Hawk that was to truly launch Honda on its quest of international fame and success. The Super Hawk had a uniquely designed twin-cyclinder engine with a chain drive to the single overhead camshaft. The engine screamed to 9000 rpm and developed 27.5 HP, which gave it a top speed of 102 to 105 mph — a speed that was superior to nearly all British 500cc models and even many of their big 650s.

Fitted with roller bearing rods and an electric starter, the Super Hawk had an engine that loved to rev and would run all day doing it. Dual carburetors and a wet sump lubrication system were used, with great pains taken to prevent oil leakage from the engine.

The chassis was also remarkable, with a well designed space frame that helped keep the weight down to 325 pounds. Full width alloy hubs were fitted with massive eight inch brakes, with the front binder having a twin leading shoe for the ultimate in braking power. Fitted with low bars and semi-rearset footpegs, the Super Hawk looked, felt, and ran like a road racer.

The American market fell in love with the Super Hawk, in both road and street-

scrambler versions. By fitting some better valvesprings, Girling shocks, and a pair of good British tires, the Super Hawk handled incredibly well and provided its rider with an experience he never forgot.

Honda's sales went straight up. By 1962 more than one million had been sold. By 1968 the figure was ten million. Honda was on his way. The world would never be the same again.

Technical Specifications

Engine:	Twin cylinder, overhead camshaft. Bore and stroke 2.3 x 2.12 inches, 305cc. Alloy cylinder and head. Roller bearing rods. Compression ratio 10.0 to 1. Two Keihin 26mm carburetors. Coil ignition. 27.5 HP at 9000 rpm.
Chassis:	Tubular, space frame, swinging arm suspension. Telescopic fork.
Transmission:	Primary and secondary chains. Foot shift. Ratios 6.27, 7.83, 10.42, and 17.48 to 1.
Tires:	2.75 x 18 inch front, 3.00 x 18 inch rear.
Brakes:	1-1/2 x 8.0 inches, drum type.
Fuel tank:	3.6 gallons.
Dimensions:	Wheelbase 51 inches. Weight 325 pounds.
Speed:	102-105 mph.

1963 Honda 50cc CR110
Japan

WHEN HONDA SHOWED up at the Isle of Man TT in 1959 with a team mounted on 125cc twins, a whole new chapter in the sport began to unfold. Prior to 1959 the only Japanese entry in the TT had been Kenza Tada, who finished in fifteenth place in the 1930 Junior TT on his Velocette, but with the entry of Honda, the Japanese were here to stay.

These first Honda racers were interesting but not taken very seriously by the Europeans. The tiny twins had a double overhead cam engine that looked suspiciously like the German 250cc NSU Renmax twins of 1954. Honda claimed 18.5 HP at 14,000 rpm for their 125, but the subsequent performance cast some doubt on this claim. The little twins did show exceptional reliability, though, with 6th, 7th, 8th, and 11th places — the fastest Honda averaging 68.29 mph compared to the 74.06 mph speed of winner Tarquinio Provini on an MV Agusta.

The engine of this first Honda racer had a bore and stroke of 41 x 41mm, two Keihin carburetors, a magneto ignition, and a wet sump lubrication system. The chassis consisted of a space frame with an orthodox swinging-arm on the rear, but up front a leading-link fork was used. The brakes were massive 180mm units, with the front having a twin leading shoe design. The front tire was a 2.50 x 18 inch size and the rear a 2.75 x 18, with the bike weighing 176 pounds.

Honda returned to Japan immediately after the TT and set about improving their racer. In August they showed up at the Asama Locano circuit with another surprise — a 250cc four that also looked suspiciously like the early 1950s NSU four-cylinder racer. The new four had a bore and stroke of 44 x 41mm, twin overhead cams, coil ignition, and four carburetors. Operating on a 10.5 to 1 compression ratio, the engine was rated at 35 HP at 14,000 rpm.

These new Hondas were interesting but hardly competitive against the European road racing bikes, so Honda once again returned to their drawing boards to design some totally new machines. In the spring of 1960 the 125cc twins and 250cc fours were shown to the world, and gone was any suggestion of copying any other design. The new racers were totally original and looked competitve.

These newest racers had engines canted forward in their frames and used four valves per cylinder — an idea used on their 1959 125cc twin. Europe had dropped the four valve concept in the early 1930s and scoffed at its use by Honda, but within one year Honda was the one laughing as the European race shops decided to stuff four valves into each combustion chamber.

The new Hondas performed well in the 1960 grand prix races but not quite fast enough to win. In 1961 they again contested the world championships, only this time their performance was so superior that they swept all before them on their way to the two championships. By then their 125cc twin was developing 25 HP at 13,000 rpm for a 112 mph speed, while the 250 four was producing 45 HP at 14,000 revs for a 137 mph speed.

1963 Honda 50cc CR110

During the following six years up to the end of the 1967 season when they pulled out of grand prix racing, Honda became the dominant force in racing with 50, 125, 250, 350, and 500cc racers with one, two, four, five, and even six cylinder engines that screamed up to 20,000 rpm. The only title they failed to win was the 500cc, where even the brilliance of Mike Hailwood could not make the 500cc four handle well enough to beat the MV.

During these years Honda produced some replica racers in only 1963 and 1964. Just small numbers of these hand-crafted racers were produced, which all had the 4-valve idea as used on the works bikes. These racers were highly successful, but by the late 1960s the two-strokes had become so fast that the Hondas became obsolete. They are now a treasured classic.

The replica racer shown here is a CR110 — a 50cc single with a twin-cam head and an eight-speed gearbox. A work of art, the miniscule thumper screamed to 14,000 rpm for 9 HP and ran 87 mph without a fairing and close to 95 with one. Weighing only 132 pounds, the CR110 was an excellent machine for the privateer who wanted to compete in the 50cc class first set up by the F.I.M. in 1962.

The power band on the CR110 was very narrow. Below seven grand the power fell to nothing. The normal power range was from 11,000 rpm to 14,500, which is why the little Honda had an eight speed box. Eight speed gearboxes weren't enough to keep the Honda competitive against the two-strokes, however, so that by 1967 they had pretty well disappeared from the tracks to become a beautiful collectable.

Technical Specifications

Engine:	Single cylinder, double overhead camshaft. Bore and stroke 40.4 x 39mm, 49cc. Alloy head and cylinder. Roller bearing rod. Compression ratio 10.3 to 1. Keihin 20mm carburetor. Coil ignition. 9 HP at 14,500 rpm.
Chassis:	Tubular, twin loop, space frame, swinging arm suspension. Telescopic fork.
Transmission:	Gear primary, secondary chain. Foot shift. Gear ratios to suit the track. Internal ratios .85, .89, .96, 1.04, 1.13, 1.32, 1.55, and 2.06 to 1.
Tires:	2.00 x 18 inch front, 2.25 x 18 inch rear.
Brakes:	1.0 x 5.3 inches, drum type.
Fuel tank:	2-1/4 gallons.
Dimensions:	Wheelbase 45 inches. Weight 132 pounds.
Speed:	87 mph.

1975 Norton 850cc Commando
England

ONE OF THE TRULY great names in the history of the motorcycle, Norton first came to fame when they won the first Isle of Man TT in 1907. This first Norton TT winner was a twin, but from then until the early 1960s, Norton was to be known for their superb OHV and OHC singles in touring, sports, and racing versions.

When Norton did decide to re-enter the twin-cylinder market in 1949, few people noticed. Everyone then was talking about the latest TT or grand prix win by the famous Manx single, or perhaps saving up their money for an International road-going replica of the racer. And then there was the venerable 500cc ES-2 OHV single that continued in production until the end of 1963 — probably the toughest and most durable motorcycle England ever built.

Norton in 1949 meant single cylinders, not twins, which is a shame since their new 500cc Model 7 Dominator twin was a very good motorcycle. With much less vibration than the big thumpers, the plunger-frame vertical-twin was a superb 90 mph roadster with typical Norton durability.

In 1953 all the Nortons appeared with a swinging-arm frame, and then in 1956 a 600cc version of the twin was produced with a 100 mph performance. Next came the 650cc Manxman in 1960, which was followed by the big 750cc Atlas in 1963. Packing a stout 50 HP, the Atlas would easily exceed 100 mph, yet it was so tractable that it would dawdle along in traffic at 20 mph on its tall 4.35 top gear.

The Atlas had a big problem, however, and this was the horrible amount of vibration that balooned handlebars at higher revs and beat the rider to death. The original old English vertical-twin design, invented in 1938 by Edward Turner, had reached its limits. The one-piece crankshaft, without a center main bearing, was just too long and out of balance to not vibrate at high revs on a long 89mm stroke.

There were two approaches Norton could take. One was to redesign the engine in some radical manner, and the other was to somehow dampen the vibration before it got to the rider. BMW used the first method in their opposed twins that have such perfect balance, and a few years later the Japanese used the smooth four-cyclinder approach to solve the problem.

Norton chose a different approach when they designed their Isolastic Suspension in which the engine, gearbox, and the pivot bearings for the swinging-arm were hooked together and then suspended from the frame by rubber bushings. The vibration was thus channeled away from the main frame and absorbed by the rear wheel and tire. The result was an amazingly smooth big vertical twin that went on to record wide public acceptance all over the world.

Norton also spent a great deal of time getting their bike to handle really well, which the new Commando did. First produced in 1968, the Commando weighed 385 pounds and would run 120 mph if properly geared. The redesigned engine with a 73 x 89mm bore and stroke

1975 Norton 850cc Commando

punched out 60 HP at 6800 rpm and would turn the standing quarter-mile in well under 13 seconds. It looked good, it handled, and it went like a bomb.

In 1972 a hotter 65 HP Combat engine was produced, as was an optional disc front brake. By then the Commando was offered in several models as a long distance tourer, a semi-custom, a sporty city-street bike, and several production racing and pure racing versions. The factory riders were very successful in 750cc class races, the endurance races, and in formula production-model events. Peter Williams lapped the TT course at over 100 mph, and Norton was back in the news again.

In 1974 Norton bored out their engine to 828cc and lowered the compression ratio to 8.5 to 1. The new engine didn't produce any more power than the 750, due partly to the new quiet mufflers that governmental regulations around the world were requiring, but it was an exceptionally flexible engine that would still run 125 mph on a tall 4.2 to 1 gear ratio. The American models were given a 4.6 to 1 ratio, however, since the British seem to think that all we do here is drag race from one stoplight to the next. With this gearing the top speed was only 114 mph, but the acceleration was shattering.

Norton then added an electric starter in

1975 — a move that increased the weight to 460 pounds and tarnished the image of fine handling. This was destined to be the final year of production, however, since a series of labor disputes led to the occupation of the Triumph factory in Meriden. In 1973 Norton had taken in the Triumph

when the Triumph Company was a part of the bankrupt BSA Company. Dennis Poore, the managing director of Norton, wanted to close the Meriden plant due to its obsolescence, but the workers objected and occupied the plant. The whole fiasco brought bankruptcy to Norton — a sad end for such an historic company. The Commando thus brought to an end over three-quarters of a century of Norton motorcycles and perhaps the greatest tradition the sport has ever known.

Technical Specifications

Engine: Twin cylinder, overhead valve. Bore and stroke 77 x 89mm, 828cc. Cast iron cylinder and alloy head. Plain bearing rods. Compression ratio 8.5 to 1. Two 32mm Amal carburetors. Coil ignition. 60 HP at 5900 rpm.

Chassis: Tubular, twin loop, isolastic frame. Telescopic fork.

Transmission: Primary and secondary chains. Foot shift. Ratios 4.6, 5.6, 7.5, and 11.8 to 1.

Tires: 4.10 x 19 inch front and rear.

Brakes: Lockhead 10.7 inch, disc type.

Fuel tank: 3.0 gallons.

Dimensions: Wheelbase 57 inches. Weight 460 pounds.

Speed: 114 to 125 mph, depending upon gear ratio.